CAGED

CAGED

NEW JERSEY PRISON
THEATER COOPERATIVE

Introductions by Chris Hedges and Boris Franklin

Haymarket Books
Chicago, Illinois

Published in 2022 by
Haymarket Books
P.O. Box 180165
Chicago, IL 60618
773-583-7884
www.haymarketbooks.org
info@haymarketbooks.org

ISBN: 978-1-64259-709-7

Distributed to the trade in the US through Consortium Book Sales
and Distribution (www.cbsd.com) and internationally through
Ingram Publisher Services International (www.ingramcontent.com).
This book was published with the generous support of Lannan
Foundation and Wallace Action Fund.

Special discounts are available for bulk purchases by organizations
and institutions. Please email info@haymarketbooks.org.

Cover artwork by Dwayne Booth, a.k.a. Mr. Fish.

Printed in Canada by union labor.
Library of Congress Cataloging-in-Publication data is available.
10 9 8 7 6 5 4 3 2 1

Caged play performances
Inquiries regarding performance rights should be addressed to:
ICM Partners
65 East 55th Street
New York, NY 10022
Attn: Ross Weiner rweiner@icmpartners.com
212-556-5798

*We have been buried alive behind these walls for years,
often decades. Most of the outside world has abandoned us.
But a few friends and family have never forgotten that we
are human beings and worthy of life. It is to them,
our saints, that we dedicate this play.*

INTRODUCTION

Chris Hedges

BEGAN TEACHING a class of twenty-eight prisoners at a maximum-security prison in New Jersey during the first week of September 2013. The course revolved around plays by August Wilson, James Baldwin, John Herbert, Tarell Alvin McCraney, Miguel Piñero, Amiri Baraka, and other playwrights who examine and give expression to the realities of America's Black underclass as well as the prison culture. We also read Michelle Alexander's important book *The New Jim Crow: Mass Incarceration in the Age of Colorblindness*. Each week the students were required to write dramatic scenes based on their experiences in and out of prison.

My class, although I did not know this when I began teaching, had the most literate and accomplished writers in the prison. And when I read the first batch of scenes it was immediately apparent that among these students was exceptional talent.

The class members had a keen eye for detail, had lived through the moral and physical struggles of prison life and had the ability to capture the patois of the urban poor and the prison underclass. They were able to portray, in dramatic scenes and dialogue, the horror of being locked in cages for years. And although the play they collectively wrote is fundamentally about radical love and sacrifice—the sacrifice of mothers for children, brothers for brothers, prisoners for prisoners—the title they chose was *Caged.* They made it clear that the traps that hold them are as present in impoverished urban communities as they are in prisons.

The mass incarceration of primarily poor people of color, people who seldom have access to adequate legal defense and who are often kept behind bars for years for nonviolent crimes or for crimes they did not commit, is one of the most shameful mass injustices committed in the United States. It is the most important civil rights issue of our time. The twenty-eight men in my class had cumulatively spent 515 years in prison. Some of their sentences were utterly disproportionate to the crimes of which they are accused. Most, five years later, are not even close to finishing their sentences or coming before a parole board, which rarely grants first-time applicants their liberty. Many of them are in for life. One of my students was arrested at the age of fourteen for a crime that strong evidence suggests he did not commit. He will not be eligible for parole until he is seventy. He never had a chance in court, and because he cannot afford a private attorney he has no chance of challenging the grotesque sentence handed to him as a child.

My stacks of twenty-eight scenes written by the students each week, the paper bearing the musty, sour smell of the prison, rose into an ungainly pile. I laboriously shaped and edited the material. It grew, line by line, scene by scene, into a powerful and deeply moving dramatic vehicle. The voices and reality of those at the very bottom rung of our society—some of the 2.3 million people in prisons and jails across the country, those we as a society are permitted to demonize and hate, just as African

Americans were demonized and hated during slavery and Jim Crow—began to flash across the pages like lightning strikes. There was more brilliance, literacy, passion, wisdom, and integrity in that classroom than in any other classroom I have taught in, and I have taught at some of the most elite universities in the country. The mass incarceration of men and women like my students impoverishes not just them, their families, and their communities but the rest of us.

"The most valuable Blacks are those in prison," August Wilson once said, "those who have the warrior spirit, who had a sense of being African. They got for their women and children what they needed when all other avenues were closed to them." He added: "The greatest spirit of resistance among Blacks [is] found among those in prison."

I increased the class meetings by one night a week. I read the scenes to my wife, Eunice Wong, who is a professional actor, and friends such as the cartoonist Joe Sacco and the theologian James Cone who said, when he finished, that he heard in the voices of the playwrights "the cries of the crucified of the earth and the liberating and radical message of the Gospel." Something unique, almost magical, was happening in the prison classroom—a place I could reach only after passing through two metal doors and a metal detector, subjecting myself to a pat-down by a corrections officer, an X-ray inspection of my canvas bag of books and papers, getting my hand stamped and then checked under an ultraviolet light, and then passing through another metal door into a barred circular enclosure. In every visit I was made to stand in the enclosure for several minutes before being permitted by the corrections officers to pass through a barred gate and then walk up blue metal stairs, through a gauntlet of blue-uniformed corrections officers, to my classroom.

The class, through the creation of the play, became an intense place of reflection, debate, and self-discovery. Offhand comments, such as the one made by a student who has spent twenty-two years behind bars, that "just because your family doesn't visit you doesn't mean they don't love you," captured the pain, loneliness, and abandonment embedded in their lives.

A student, a product of rape, with nineteen years behind bars read his half of a phone dialogue between himself and his mother. He tells his mother that he sacrificed himself to keep his half-brother—the only son he believes his mother loves—out of prison. He read this passage in the final reading of the play in the prison chapel.

TERRANCE: You don't understand, Ma.

   Pause.

TERRANCE: You're right. Never mind.

   Pause.

TERRANCE: What you want me to say, Ma?

   Pause.

TERRANCE: Ma, they were going to lock up Bruce. The chrome [the gun] was in the car. Everyone in the car would be charged with murder if no one copped to it . . .

   Pause.

TERRANCE: I didn't kill anyone, Ma . . . Oh yeah, I forgot, whenever someone says I did, I did it.

   Pause.

TERRANCE: I told 'em what they wanted to hear. That's what

niggas supposed to do in Newark. I told them what they
wanted to hear to keep Bruce out of it. Did they tell you
who got killed? Did they say it was my father?
Pause.

TERRANCE: Then you should know I didn't do it. If I ever went
to jail for anything it would be killing him . . . and he ain't
dead yet. Rape done brought me into the world. Prison
gonna take me out. An' that's the way it is, Ma.
Pause.

TERRANCE: Come on Ma, if Bruce went to jail you would've
never forgiven me. Me, on the other hand, I wasn't ever
supposed to be here.
Pause.

TERRANCE: I'm sorry Ma . . . I'm sorry. Don't be cryin'. You got
Bruce. You got him home. He's your baby. Bye, Ma. I'll call
you later.

When he finished he disappeared from the stage. I found
him, hunched over in a corner of the bathroom, sobbing.

After Boris Franklin, perhaps my strongest writ-
er, was released from prison in 2015 we worked together to reshape the play. This meant merging and cutting
the twenty-eight roles, one for each of my students, into
a more manageable cast and adding character depth and
complexity. We were forced to cut a lot of powerful material, including this phone dialogue. But the play, as it was
originally written, was more concerned with giving every
student a voice than functioning as a dramatic production. Boris and I, along with Eunice and the director Jeff
Wise, who organized workshops for the play in New York

that were vital in bringing it to life, honed and edited the play until it could be staged.

In the play, when a young prisoner contemplates killing another prisoner, he is given advice on how to survive prolonged isolation in the management control unit (solitary confinement, known as MCU) by an older prisoner who has spent thirty years in prison under a sentence of double life. In the United States there are eighty-thousand prisoners held in solitary confinement, which human rights organizations such as Amnesty International define as a form of torture. In this scene the older man tells the young inmate what to expect from the corrections officers (COs).

OJORE (*SPEAKING SLOWLY AND SOFTLY*): When they come and get you, 'cause they are gonna get you, have your hands out in front of you with your palms showing. You want them to see you have no weapons. Don't make no sudden moves. Put your hands behind your head. Drop to your knees as soon as they begin barking out commands.

OMAR: My knees?

OJORE: This ain't a debate. I'm telling you how to survive the hell you 'bout to endure. When you get to the hole you ain't gonna be allowed to have nothing but what they give you. If you really piss them off you get a 'dry cell' where the sink and the toilet are turned on and off from outside. You gonna be isolated. No contact. No communication.

OMAR: Why?

OJORE: 'Cause they don't want you sendin' messages to nobody before dey question some of da brothers on the wing. IA

[Internal Affairs officers] gonna come and see you. They gonna want a statement. If you don't talk they gonna try and break you. They gonna open the windows and let the cold in. They gonna take ya sheets and blankets away. They gonna mess with ya food so you can't eat it. An' don't eat no food that come in trays from the Vroom Building. Nuts in Vroom be spittin', pissin', and shittin' in the trays. Now, the COs gonna wake you up every hour on the hour so you can't sleep. They gonna put a bright-ass spotlight in front of ya cell and keep it on day and night. They gonna harass you wit' all kinds of threats to get you to cooperate. They will send in the turtles in their shin guards, gloves, shank-proof vests, forearm guards and helmets with plexiglass shields on every shift to give you beatdowns.

OMAR: How long this gonna go on?

OJORE: 'Til they break you. Or 'til they don't. Three days. Three weeks. You don't break, it go on like this for a long time. An' if you don't think you can take it, then don't start puttin' yerself through this hell. Just tell 'em what they wanna know from the door. You gonna be in MCU for the next two or three years. You'll get indicted for murder. You lookin' at a life bid. An' remember MCU ain't jus' 'bout isolation. It's 'bout keeping you off balance. The COs, dressed up in riot gear, wake you up at 1 a.m., force you to strip and make you grab all your things and move you to another cell just to harass you. They bring in dogs trained to go for your balls. You spend twenty-four hours alone one day in your cell and twenty-two the next. They put you in the MCU and wait for you to self-destruct. An' it works. Men self-mutilate. Men get paranoid. Men have panic attacks. They start hearing voices. They talk crazy to themselves. I seen one prisoner swallow a pack of AA batteries. I seen a man shove a pencil up his dick. I seen men toss human shit around like it was a ball game. I seen men eat their own shit and rub it all over themselves like it was some kinda body lotion. Then, when you really get out of control, when you go really crazy, they got all their torture instruments ready—four- and five-point restraints, restraint hoods, restraint belts, restraint beds, stun grenades, stun guns, stun belts, spit hoods, tethers, and waist and leg chains. But the physical stuff ain't the worst. The worst is the psychological, the humiliation, sleep deprivation, sensory disorientation, extreme light or dark, extreme cold or heat and the long weeks and months of solitary. If you don't have a strong sense of purpose you don't survive. They want to defeat you mentally. An' I seen a lot of men defeated.

THE VARIOUS drafts of the play, made up of scenes and dialogue contributed by everyone in the class, brought to the surface the suppressed emotions and pain that the students bear with profound stoicism and dignity. A prisoner who has been incarcerated for twenty-two years related a conversation with his wife during her final visit in 1997. Earlier, his six-year-old son had innocently revealed that the woman was seeing another man. "I am aware of what kind of time I got," he tells his wife. "I told you when I got found guilty to move on with your life, because I knew what kind of time I was facing, but you chose to stick around. The reason I told you to move on with your life was because I didn't want to be selfish. So look, man, do what the fuck you are going to do, just don't keep my son from me. That's all I ask." He never saw his child again. When I asked him if he would read it to the class his eyes welled with tears and he choked out: "I can't."

Those with life sentences wrote about dying in prison. The prisoners are painfully aware that some of them will end their lives in the medical wing without family, friends, or even former cellmates. One prisoner, who wrote about how men in prolonged isolation adopt prison mice as pets, naming them, carefully bathing them, talking to them, and keeping them on string leashes, worked in the prison infirmary. He said that as some prisoners were dying they would ask him to hold their hand. Often no one comes to collect the bodies. Often, family members and relatives are dead or long estranged. The corpses are taken by the prison authorities and dumped in unmarked graves.

A discussion of Wilson's play *Fences* became an exploration of damaged manhood and how patterns of abuse are passed down from father to son. "I spent my whole life trying not to be my father," a prisoner who has been locked up for twenty-three years said. "And when I got to Trenton I was put in his old cell."

The night we spoke about the brilliant play *Dutchman*, by LeRoi Jones, now known as Amira Baraka, the class grappled with whites' deeply embedded stereotypes and latent fear of Black men. I had also passed out copies of Robert Crumb's savage cartoon strip "When the Niggers Take Over America!," which portrays whites' fear of Black males—as well as the understandable Black rage that is rarely understood by white society.

The students wanted to be true to the violence and brutality of the streets and prison—places where one does not usually have the luxury of being nonviolent—yet affirm themselves as dignified and sensitive human beings. They did not want to paint everyone in the prison as innocents. But they know that transformation and redemption are real.

There are many Muslims in the prison. They have a cohesive community, sense of discipline, and knowledge of their own history, which is the history of the long repression and subjugation of African Americans. Most Muslims are very careful about their language in prison and do not curse, meaning I had to be careful when I assigned parts to the class.

There is a deep reverence in the prison for Malcolm X. When the class spoke of him one could almost feel Malcolm's presence. Malcolm articulated, in a way Martin Luther King Jr. did not, the harsh reality of poor African Americans trapped in the internal colonies of the urban North.

The class wanted the central oracle of the play to be an observant Muslim. Faith, when you live in the totalitarian world of the prison, is often vital. The conclusion of the play was the result of an intense and heated discussion about the efficacy and nature of violence and forgiveness. But by the end of a nearly hour-long discussion the class had unanimously signed off on the final scene. Their capacity for radical love was the core message the prisoners wanted most to leave with outsiders, who often view them as less than human.

The play has a visceral, raw anger and undeniable truth that only the lost and the damned can articulate. The students wrote a dedication that read: "We have been buried alive behind these walls for years, often decades. Most of the outside world has abandoned us. But a few friends and family have never forgotten that we are human beings and worthy of life. It is to them, our saints, that we dedicate this play."

We read the Wilson play *Joe Turner's Come and Gone.* The character Bynum Walker, a conjurer, tells shattered African Americans emerging from the nightmare of slavery that they each have a song but they must seek it out. Once they find their song they will find their unity as a people, their inner freedom, and their identity. The search for one's song in Wilson's play functions like prayer. It gives each person purpose, strength, and hope. It allows a person, even one who has been bitterly oppressed, to speak his or her truth defiantly to the world. Our song affirms us, even if we are dejected and despised, as human beings.

Prisoners are given very little time by the corrections officers to line up in the corridor outside the classroom when the prison bell signals the end of class. If they lag behind they can get a "charge" that can restrict their already very limited privileges and freedom of movement. For this reason, my classroom emptied quickly the last Friday night. I was left alone in the empty space, my eyes damp, my hands trembling as I clutched their manuscript. They had all signed the cover page for me. I made the long and lonely walk down the prison corridors, through the four metal security doors, past the security desk to the dark, frozen parking lot. I looked back, past the coils of razor wire that topped the chain-link fencing, at the shadowy bulk of the prison. I held their song. Now it will be heard.

This introduction was adapted from a column called "The Play's the Thing" published by Truthdig *on December 16, 2013.*

INTRODUCTION

Boris Franklin

FOR ELEVEN years I was one of 2.3 million Americans incarcerated in our prison system. Prison is its own culture. It comes with its own peculiar set of norms, behaviors, and rules. If you are poor and Black, however, you are conditioned for prison in dysfunctional and overcrowded schools where in the morning you are greeted with metal detectors and police and where in the yard there are fights. You live in dangerous, run-down housing projects, whose smell and decay are replicated in moldering prisons. You navigate the streets in deindustrialized wastelands where despair is rampant and the exit doors of drugs, alcohol, crime, and violence are ubiquitous. You are hauled in front of courts to face lists of charges invented by the police, who oversee mini reigns of terror in your neighborhood, to force you to plea out. Few of the incarcerated ever get a jury trial. The justice system does not work for us. Prison was not a huge culture shock for me. And it was not a huge culture shock for most of the brothers I did time with. In America they prepare you for your future.

Once you are in prison the state seeks to erase your identity, forcing you—when you first enter—to strip while your body is searched, a public humiliation endlessly repeated until the day you are released. The state not only takes away your dignity and freedom, making you sleep and live in a cage, it takes away your name, replacing it with a number. You are forced to give up your rights as a citizen, limited as they were. You are dressed in prison khakis to look like everyone else. You are allowed few possessions, and these can be and are confiscated from you, often on the whim of a guard. There are no conjugal visits. You lose, if you are a heterosexual, your identity as a sexual being, part of the reason for the exaggerated homophobia in male prisons. You cannot move without permission, and when you do move it is usually in a military-style formation with other prisoners. You stand for head counts. You are under constant surveillance. You cannot leave your cell without permission. The word of the guard is law. Your word is worthless. At any point the administration can send in a squad of heavily protected guards (we call them the "turtles") to beat and bind you in restraints and send you to solitary confinement. Solitary confinement is designed to break you psychologically if the guards deem you need to be broken. The guards use it on anyone who attempts to rebel, organize prisoner opposition—even nonviolent opposition—to prison rules, and on anyone who is insufficiently obsequious to authority. If you get a job you are paid twenty-two cents an hour or about twenty-eight dollars a month, funds drained from you by the for-profit commissary, for-profit medical care, for-profit telephone, and for-profit money transfer services. Corporations make billions by exploiting the most vulnerable. Prisoners can leave prison in debt. Families struggle to get a little money to loved ones on the inside. These constant assaults on your being, including being reduced to pleading for money from your family and friends on the outside, shake your confidence in yourself. And they are meant to.

Hierarchies are formed and encouraged by the prison administrators to turn the prisoners against each other. Runners with good disciplinary records can roam the prison carrying out tasks. Snitches collaborate with the guards for small privileges. Sexual predators abuse other men, usually the young who in prison slang are called "new fish." The leaders of cliques, gangs, or groups organize to control and oppress others, often by demanding they surrender commissary items or a privileged job. And then there are the killers, the real killers, of whom there are surprisingly few in a prison, who everyone stays away from. As the United States devolves into a system where the ruling elites have total power, it behooves those on the outside to look closely at what the state has done to those of us in the inside.

You struggle to adapt to this system, which is in essence totalitarian, as best you can. If you are a person with integrity you don't sell your brothers out, you try to help those who are struggling emotionally or who have no one on the outside to send them some money, and you resist letting the state turn you into a zombie, which is its goal. You don't publicly show grief or excessive emotion. As my friend Ron Pierce said, "This is a house of grief. The brothers can't take any more grief. You got to grieve alone." You don't ask a brother what he is in for. You don't talk much about your life on the outside. The less people know about you the better. You keep your emotions and your history to yourself. You don't touch, and if you bump into someone, assuming you are not looking for a fight, you are profusely apologetic. Prisoners can be the politest people on earth.

The most powerful prisoners are not the gangsters. They are those who have earned the respect of the other prisoners and the guards. There is less violence in a well-run prison than many on the outside assume, since it is the word and stature of these prison leaders that creates social cohesion. These leaders ward off conflicts between prisoners, raise issues of concern with the administrators, and intercede with the guards. They intuitively understand how to navigate the narrow parameters set by prison authorities, giving them something that resembles freedom. Prison is a lot like the outside world. There is a stratum of people you try to avoid. There are the majority who spend most of their free time slack-jawed in front of a television set, and then there are those who have recovered their integrity and even, to an extent, their moral autonomy. They have risen above prison to become better people. Yet, even they can be arbitrarily disappeared into solitary confinement or shipped to another prison by the administration. Everyone in prison is disposable.

It was this last group of twenty-eight prisoners that Professor Chris Hedges met when he walked into a prison classroom in Rahway, New Jersey in September 2013. These were some of the 140 men who comprised what we called Rahway University, those of us who dedicated all our free time to studying to earn our college degree. We would be in the yard working the pile talking about Plato or Augustine. We exchanged ideas about the readings from our bunks or in the mess hall. And we tutored those who were falling behind. We had converted our cells into libraries. Our books were our most precious possessions, especially since we had to scrape together the money to buy them. We did not lend them unless we were sure they would be read and even surer they would be returned. And if you read one of our books you had better be prepared to give an intelligent commentary on its contents. We were a dedicated fraternity of prison scholars.

We had all taken classes before in the college program run by the New Jersey Scholarship and Transformative Education in Prisons Consortium (NJ STEP) through Rutgers University, but this class would be unique. It would shatter the prison's unwritten rules of comportment. It would open us to each other in ways we had never been open before, even though many of us had lived together for years. It would give us a voice, finally, outside the prison walls.

All this was not by design. Professor Hedges, when he first arrived in the classroom intending to teach a course on drama, did not initially propose writing a play. His goal was to make us familiar with dramatic form, which most of us were not. He wanted us to read the plays by August Wilson, James Baldwin, Amiri Baraka and others, and learn to think and write in the language of theater.

He asked us to write about our experiences, and those of our families, outside of prison as well as our life in prison in dramatic dialogue. We reached back into our past to produce small dramatic scenes. We resurrected emotions and painful experiences, as well as ones of joy and love, buried deep within us. Professor Hedges selected several dialogues each week to read out loud, sometimes asking the student who wrote it to read it to the class. There were many times, however, when the pain of what had been put down on the paper was too much to speak.

Two or three weeks into the course Professor Hedges said he thought the writing by many of us was strong enough to put together a play of our life outside prison, where the cages are not always visible, and inside prison. He would work as our editor, but we would be the final authority on the script. He was allowed under the prison rules to come in a second day a week to offer tutorial help to those who needed it. He signed us all up for tutorial help.

Stories of pain, humiliation, humor, love, courage, grief, loneliness, loss, shame, and guilt poured out of us. The emotional walls erected between us in the prison began to crumble. And as we listened to these stories being read out loud, often by men whose voices were breaking with emotion, we began to understand that when you are a poor person of color in America you have one story. There are different variations of this story. But the core is the same, one made familiar by white supremacy, poverty, neglect, despair, rage, violence, addictions, and abandonment. Telling this story, our story, was liberating. We found our voice. Our voice became the play *Caged*.

It was the class none of us ever wanted to end. It was a strange form of therapy. Men in the class bonded. They saw themselves in their brothers' eyes. They learned to speak the unspeakable. When we first started writing the play only seven people wanted parts. By the end, all twenty-eight students wanted a role. There was almost nothing set down on paper that a member of the class did not experience or witness. It was a work of collective fiction that presented a universal truth. We fiercely debated the narrative of *Caged*, especially the ending of the play when there is a choice between honoring the prison code of vengeance and violence or rising above it. Professor Hedges promised us that he would work to find a theater willing to stage this universal truth. Many people make promises to prisoners. Few people keep them.

In the spring of 2015, I was released from prison. Professor Hedges, along with my mother, my sister, and my daughters, were at the prison gate. I was the only one from the class who was on the outside. We could not mount a play with twenty-eight parts. Characters had to be cut and consolidated. Many characters needed more dramatic depth, especially among the family members who open the play and who carry the narrative. Professor Hedges and I began to take the raw script and shape it into a script that would work on stage. But we were both acutely aware that we were not playwrights.

We submitted scenes to Eunice Wong, a professional actor who is married to Professor Hedges, and she sent them back with critiques that often required us to begin all over again. The New York theater director Jeff Wise reached out to us and offered to fund and hold workshops in New York with professional actors, so we could try out versions of the script and see what worked and what did not. We invited critics, including the theologian James Cone and movie director Marty Brest along with other formerly incarcerated people, to come to the readings and give us feedback. We brought in other writers who had been incarcerated and helped with the script, especially Ojore Latulo, Ron Pierce, and Serena Green, so we could include the experience of incarcerated women, who usually have it harder than the men. The characters and scenes in Jeff's workshops were closely examined, critiqued, and reconstructed. The script evolved, and the characters came alive. It took on nuance and complexity. We began to have a play.

We based many of the scenes, especially those involving the Moore family in the play, on my own family. I grew up with a devout Christian mother and a father who was a hustler and drug addict. I rolled myself and my siblings into the three siblings in the play. I sought to create the emotional complexity and family dynamics that give expression to the radical love which is at the heart of the play. The play, if you examine it closely, is really about self-sacrifice for those we love. Often this self-sacrifice cannot save those we love given the unforgiving world we live in. This makes the effort at once noble and tragic.

In May of 2018 the play was performed at The Passage Theater in Trenton, New Jersey. It was sold out nearly every night. Mass incarceration has wounded many people in Trenton as it has in most depressed urban areas in America. I took one of the roles. The rest were filled by professional actors. Every night I heard the voices of these men, men I spent many years with and care deeply about. Some of these men will die in prison. This is a story that rarely gets told. It is told by the victims, or those the Dr. Cone calls "the crucified of the earth." The ability to have a voice on the outside validates prisoners as human beings worthy of being heard. The play—its writing and production—filled the dead and oppressive weight of prison time with an act of creation, self-expression, and meaning.

There are plays written about prison, but very few plays written by prisoners. Too often our voices are interpreted for the outside world by others. In *Caged* you hear an unvarnished, raw truth and see the dignity of the oppressed. The structural, racist forces that keep the poor poor, are ever-present in the play. These forces define, and for centuries have defined, the struggle of Black families in America. They are too often unseen and unacknowledged by those on the outside, but, in this play, they are as present as the characters who appear onstage.

CAGED was produced by The Passage Theater (C. Ryanne Domingues, artistic director; Damion A. Parran, managing director) in Trenton, New Jersey, on May 3, 2018. It was directed by Jerrell L. Henderson; the set design was by Germán Cárdenas-Alaminos; the lighting design was by Daniel Schreckengost; the sound design was by Beth Lake; the costume design was by An-lin Dauber; the production design was by Miranda Kelly; the production stage manager was Laura Marsh; the production coordinator was Dan Viola. The cast was as follows:

Jimmy Moore/Ojore . . . . Will Badgett

Shorty/Various . . . . Andrew Binger

Officer Watkins/Slash/Social Worker . . . . Boris Franklin

Quan Moore . . . . Ural Grant

Sharonda Moore . . . . Nicolette Lynch

Omar Moore . . . . Brandon Rubin

Chimene Moore . . . . Monah Yancy

CHARACTERS

CHIMENE MOORE: A Black woman in her fifties. Thin and
tired as a result of her long struggle with breast cancer.
She is endowed with an inner strength that makes her
majestic. She is the mother of Omar, Sharonda, and Quan.

OMAR MOORE: A powerfully built Black man about thirty. He
wears jeans and a T-shirt and no flashy jewelry. He once
oversaw most of the drug dealing in the neighborhood,
but left with his family to live in Georgia. He has come
back after four years away and is rebuilding his drug trade.

QUAN MOORE: Sixteen. He is the younger brother of Omar.
His brother and mother have protected him from the
streets. Omar is his father figure.

SHARONDA MOORE: Omar and Quan's twenty-year-old sister.

JIMMY MOORE: Father of Omar, Quan, and Sharonda and
husband of Chimene. In his fifties. A junkie. Charming,
quick-witted, and funny when he wants to be, he can also
swiftly turn menacing, cruel, and frightening. It is clear in
the way he carries himself that he is capable of violence.

BLOOD MONEY: A prisoner in Essex County Jail.

OFFICER WATKINS: A middle-aged Black man, built like an
out-of-shape heavyweight boxer. He has worked in the
prison intake unit for more than a decade.

OJORE ABU SHARIF: A long-time prisoner in Scarborough
State for the murder of two Newark policemen in a bank
robbery. He is a revolutionary grounded in the radical

ideology of the Black power movement of 1960s. Ojore was an armed member of the Black Liberation Army. He spent twenty-two years in solitary confinement and has been recently released to the general population. A devout Muslim, he is fair, open, and endowed with gravitas, but it is also clear from his physical presence that he is not to be crossed.

MR. CHARLIE: An elderly Black prisoner in Scarborough State Prison.

THEO "SHORTY" TERRELL: A Black man of about eighteen. He is a low-level drug dealer and drug user in Newark.

NEWARK POLICE OFFICER 1

NEWARK POLICE OFFICER 2

ADDICT: A dope addict in his thirties, disheveled and poorly dressed.

ALAMEEN: An older prisoner in the county jail.

DARYL STOKES: a.k.a. Slash or Uncle Bip: sixties, Omar's godfather. In Scarborough State Prison for a double life sentence. A devout Muslim.

SHAKY BROWN: A gifted blues musician serving a life sentence in Scarborough.

PRISON GUARDS: One and Two at Funeral Home.

SOCIAL WORKER

Playwrights on the Inside (as of 2013)

LAWRENCE BELL: Camden. 24 years in prison. Eligible for parole at age 70 in 2045. Incarcerated at the age of 14.

GENE BERTA: Edison. 30 years in prison. Eligible for parole in

2014. Navy veteran. He served as a hospital corpsman. The father of seven children.

LEONARDO BUCCHERI: Jersey City. 13 years in prison. Eligible for parole in 2022 at age 53. The father of a beautiful girl and boy.

THOMAS DOLLARD: Newark. 23 years in prison. Eligible for parole in 2021 at age 51. Son of Zuberi B. Bandeie and Willa Dollard.

RONNIE FEDO: Jefferson. 20 years in prison. Eligible for parole in 2032 at age 55. Never been married. No children. Graduated from high school in 1995.

BORIS FRANKLIN: New Brunswick. 11 years in prison. Eligible for parole in May 2015. Father of four. Assistant director of the New Directions program for prisoners.

SHAHEED GULLY: Newark. 16 years in prison. Eligible for parole in 2016 at age 38. Arrested at the age of 18.

JACINTO HIGHTOWER: Willingboro. 28 years in prison. Ex-husband. Ex-father. Ex-soldier, US Army. 11 years on death row. Eligible for parole in 2015.

DE-VON HOLLOMAN: Newark. 11 years in prison. Eligible for parole in 2017. For my son Je'von. I've changed for you. For my mother, Kathy Holloman. For my beautiful wife, Amira Hubbard Holloman. Loyalty is royalty.

REGGIE "SINCERE" JACKSON: Paterson. 17 years in prison. Eligible for parole in 2037 at age 68. Father of Pilar L. Jackson. Son of Mary E. Riggins. Sentenced to a prison term of life plus 40 years, 115 years, with a 50-year parole ineligibility.

BRIAN JENKINS: 11 years in prison. Eligible for parole in 2028 at age 50. Was once lost and without hope, but found hope through the blood of Jesus.

ANTHONY LEAHEY: Plainfield. 18 years in prison. Release date 2029 at age 52. Arrested at the age of 18. Learned to read and write in prison at 20. Self-taught musician. Wrote the the music for the play.

JAMES LEAK: Elizabeth. 21 years in prison. Eligible for parole in 2024 at age 55. I am a Muslim striving to get closer to Allah, as I also continue to fight to regain freedom to be a better leader for my family during these days and times.

ROBERT LUMA: Newark. 11 years in prison. Release date 2019 at age 34. Arrested the age of 18. Found freedom behind bars.

DOMINGO MANN: Paterson. 24 years in prison. Serving 30 years to life. Eligible for parole in 2021. President of the Lifers Group. Writes poetry.

OMAR MCNEIL: Newark. 14 years in prison. Eligible for parole in 2016 at age 35. Arrested at the age of 18.

SAMMY MOORE: Newark. 21 years in prison on a 45-years-to-life sentence. Eligible for parole in 2033 at age 63. Incarcerated at 19. Hopes one day to do prison ministry.

SAMUEL QUILES: Queens. 21 years in prison. Eligible for parole in 2023 at age 47. Arrested at the age of 17. A son, an uncle, a husband, the father of a little girl, and a proud Puerto Rican.

FERNANDO ROSARIO: Trenton. 12 years in prison. Eligible for parole in 2018 at age 36. Arrested at the age of 19. Looks forward to the day he can again be with his beautiful mother, Ani.

DAVID RUSSO: Brooklyn. 28 years in prison. A 12-year veteran of the Air Force. Eligible for parole in 2025. The father of two wonderful children.

HABEEB SCOTT: Newark. 15 years in prison. Eligible for parole in 2024 at age 45. The father of Kayla Monec Scott. A Muslim.

TIMMY SMITH (FORMERLY TERRANCE BANKS): Paterson. 19 years in prison. Conceived by rape in South Carolina. Raised back and forth between the calm of the country and Paterson. Eligible for parole in 2025 at age 52. Arrested at the age of 20.

MARVIN SPEARS: Irvington. 22 years in prison. Army veteran. Eligible for parole in 2020 at the age of 55. The father of Ta'Nazia Spears.

HASHIM STOKES: Newark. 22 years in prison. Eligible for parole in 2021. From the 7th Avenue Projects. Father of Nadiyh. Son of Marie Stokes.

RA'ZULU UKAWABUTU: Atlantic City. 23 years in prison. Eligible for parole in 2024 at age 55. Father of three, Samira Stewart, Shameek Stewart, and Shawn Ra'Zulu Chambers.

HECTOR VALENTIN: Newark. 24 years in prison. Eligible for parole in 2019 at age 47. Arrested at the age of 17.

JASSON WILKINS: Trenton. 19 years in prison. Paroled in 2018 at age 46. The father of two daughters, Destinee and N'zinga, who have never experienced a day of their father's freedom.

STEPHEN WILLIAMS: Newark. 15 years in prison. Eligible for parole in 2018 at age 45. Father of Ayannah Hunter-Ali,

SaKinah M. Banks, Javonte' Jackson, Stephan Banks, and Keon Hunter.

Playwrights on the Outside

SERENA GREEN: Trenton. Jailed for 44 days because of an outstanding warrant for an old DWI.

RON PIERCE: Bayonne. 31 years in prison. Graduated summa cum laude from Rutgers University in 2018.

OJORE LUTALO: Newark. After spending 28 years in prison, he was released from New Jersey's Trenton State Penitentiary on August 26, 2009. He spent twenty-two of those years in solitary confinement in the management control unit. Member of the Black Liberation Army.

CAGED

Fifteen minutes before the play begins SHAKY BROWN,
*seated inside a barred cell that looms over the set, plays
blues. The light on the cell is dim. His music trails off
shortly before the play opens.*
Projection: ZAIRE *at age two.*

Act I, Scene I

BUILDING A BASE

---

*Late afternoon. QUAN and OMAR in a dingy room in
SHORTY's apartment. OMAR has a happy face plastic bag
with a brown paper insert (Chinese takeout) and a black
duffel bag.*

QUAN: We gonna do this here?

OMAR: Yeah, why? Grab me a plate.

> *OMAR takes a small ziplock bag of cocaine, a box of razors,
> two boxes of plastic sandwich bags, and scissors out of the
> duffel.*

QUAN (*HANDING OMAR A PLATE*): What's all this for?

OMAR: I'm goin' show you how to bag up the work. You're
only doin' this while Shorty's in the county.

QUAN: Ok.

OMAR: I'm serious, Quan. This shit ain't for you. You stay in
school.

QUAN (*INDICATING THE PLASTIC BAG*): And what's that?

OMAR: That's lunch.

> *OMAR uses the razor to cut small pieces of cocaine from the
> larger rock.*

OMAR: See that? That's a twenty-cent piece. You don't put no
more in the bag than that.

> *OMAR continues cutting and places the small rocks in the
> corners of the sandwich bags. He hands the bags to QUAN,*

who also starts cutting.

OMAR: Tie the tops of the bags an' cut off the extra plastic.

They work in silence for a few beats, QUAN *stealing glances at his older brother. Then . . .*

QUAN: Yo, why'd you come back? I thought you liked it down South.

OMAR: Yeah, little bro, you right. I wanted to get as far away from this shit as I could. I wanted to raise Zaire different.

QUAN: But you done good in the hood.

OMAR (*LAUGHS*)**:** Yeah, I did. Yo, I was younger than you when I started doin' this shit. But it gets old . . . the husslin', the money, the cars, even the girls, all that shit gets old.

QUAN: I don't know 'bout that . . .

OMAR: I know one thing . . . you gonna get old. . . . The streets stay fast. We get slow.

QUAN: So, you slow?

OMAR: Yeah, 'cause I care. You so fucked up when you start you don't care about nothin'. That's the energy . . . hit a motherfucker over the head with a stick!

Pause.

But when you start to care about shit, then you fucked. You sixteen. I got a kid. Little nigga running 'round in Star Wars pajamas.

QUAN: I bet you was mad bored in the country.

OMAR: Nah, I loved it.

QUAN: Word?

OMAR: Word up. I didn't have to look over my shoulder. Strangers would say "hi" to you. There's another world out there. Wished I could have stayed . . . In the end tho', I was out of the game, but the game wasn't out of me.

QUAN: What you mean?

OMAR: When I copped those five years of probation I didn't know it was a trap. That snake-ass prosecutor knew what he was doin'. I thought no jail time, that's what's up. But I didn't know it meant the end of jobs. I was tryin' to live on eight dollars an hour an' I was only workin' part-time . . . you can't survive on that. All that shit brings you back.

QUAN: So, you gonna get out again?

OMAR: That's the plan. Take my little man an' blow.

QUAN: Why don't you start a business? Wakeem's got a store on Broad and Market.

OMAR: That store ain't makin' shit. You know the motherfucker makin' money when he stops selling drugs. Wakeem still husslin'. He's payin' $3,000 a month jus' in rent . . . building inspector come in and tell him he got to get up to code, give him a list of things he got to fix before he open his doors. He's in a space nobody wants . . . got him at the end of the block . . . ain't nobody goin' down there to buy clothes. . . then he got the light bill . . . the phone bill . . . the people he hired. That's why all of em' with storefronts still selling drugs. They'd be better off if they opened the storefront like a trap house and sold drugs straight out. As long as they pretend they sellin' clothes they losin'.

QUAN: One day you and me gonna start a business.

OMAR: An' little bro, what business would that be?

QUAN: A bowlin' alley!

OMAR (*LAUGHING*): Ok, Quan. You be bowling all day and I be behind the counter handing out shoes.

Beat. OMAR gets down to business.

OMAR: Right now this the only business we got Quan . . . A lot of things in this world ain't right and this is one of 'em. But we don't get a lot of options. Look at Daddy. He wanted to make something of himself up North, an' they broke him like they broke Denise. I found Daddy last week in the bathroom with a needle in his arm. I had to carry him to the sofa. Here, you starting with a G pack. That's twenty dollars a rock. Post up. Be on point for 5-0 because you get locked up Mommy gonna lose her fuckin' mind.

QUAN: Some of those junkies real mean . . .

OMAR: I be right up the street. Ain't nothin' gonna happen while I here.

QUAN: What if we see Push?

OMAR: I'll handle Push.

QUAN: He don't like that you got back in the game. Says you stealin' his business . . .

OMAR: Push talk big. That was my game before he run these streets.

QUAN: They found Kareem Johnson last night back of the projects . . . seventeen gunshot wounds an' his head blown off with a shotgun . . . say he stole money from Push.

OMAR: I handle punks a lot tougher than Push.

Beat.

QUAN: I remember when Kareem's father come home from jail . . . I was in the seventh grade . . . we was sittin' in the classroom. Somebody say, 'Kareem, that's yer daddy's outside.' Kareem hadn't seen his daddy for five years. He looked like Floyd Mayweather . . . leather jacket . . . bald head . . . goatee. Kareem so excited . . . He can't stop talkin' bout his daddy. A few months later we're walking home from school and this crackhead runs up to him and says, 'Little Kareem, they just locked your daddy up. He cut somebody's throat down in the projects.' Kareem jus' shut down. Next thing you know he fightin' everybody . . .

Pause.

You still drivin' that forklift in da warehouse?

OMAR: I got laid off. But I got to give mommy something for food, rent, and her meds. That was hard workin' and hustlin,' an now I jus' hustlin.' An' Daddy ain't no help . . .

OMAR: Jus' keep out of his way. He got more bark than bite.

QUAN: He gettin' worse . . .

OMAR: The one person he ain't never gonna cross is mommy. You be a'ight . . .

Pause.

I got to take Mommy at seven in da morning for her chemo. Pick up her meds at the Rite Aid on the way home from school. Make sure you put it right in the fridge. I got a box in there with all her syringes and shit.

OMAR opens his wallet and hands QUAN some money.

This is for Ma's medicine. I got to git to sleep. I'll be stayin' here at Shorty's tonight. An' you don't go out on that street unless I'm with you. Shorty be out in two or three days an' you drop this shit. I don't want you messed up in this game.

Act I, Scene II

CHIMENE'S BLESSING

_____

Early evening. CHIMENE *is in a rocker, singing to a toddler in his bed.*

CHIMENE (*SINGING*):

> Go down, Moses
> Way down in Egypt land
> Tell all pharaohs to
> Let my people go!
> When Israel was in Egypt land
> Let my people go!
> Oppressed so hard they could not stand
> Let my people go!

SHARONDA walks into the room quietly.

CHIMENE:

> So, the God said: Go down, Moses
> Way down in Egypt land
> Tell all pharaohs to
> Let my people go!
> So Moses went to Egypt land
> Let my people go!
> He made all pharaohs understand
> Let my people go!

SHARONDA and CHIMENE speaking quietly.

SHARONDA: Zaire asleep?

CHIMENE: I think so.

SHARONDA: I love hearin' you sing, Mama.

CHIMENE: My grandma sang this to me. An' her grandma sang it to her. An' before that a mama, blood of my blood, sang it to her little girl or boy gowin' up in slavery . . . an' all these mamas had to fight the evil in the world was love . . . an' song . . .

A police siren is heard outside. CHIMENE walks to the window and looks outside.

CHIMENE: Omar home?

SHARONDA: Not yet. We got to wait? I'm gettin' hungry. You never know when he get here.

CHIMENE: He be here soon.

The light rises faintly on SHAKY BROWN's cell, and he joins CHIMENE in the song.

> Yes, the Lord said: go down, Moses
> Way down in Egypt land
> Tell all pharaohs to
> Let my people go!

The light in SHAKY BROWN's cell dims to darkness.

Sound of a door opening downstairs. SHARONDA leaves.

OMAR (*OS*): Ma?

CHIMENE leaves the window and joins OMAR in the kitchen.

OMAR: Hey, Ma. (*OMAR gives her a hug.*) Where's Zaire at?

CHIMENE: I jus' put him to bed. What's that on your face son? (*She lightly touches his face.*) You got cut.

OMAR: It's nothin', Ma. The other guy looks a lot worse.

CHIMENE (*CALLING UPSTAIRS*): Quan, time to eat. Omar's home.

OMAR: I'm goin' to say goodnight to my little man . . .

CHIMENE: Don't wake him up . . .

OMAR leaves the kitchen and heads upstairs.

SHARONDA: I seen Denise on Mulberry Street. She's trickin' for Prince. She looks like a ghost. She gave me twenty dollars for Zaire . . .

CHIMENE: I don't want that girl in the house.

SHARONDA: She Zaire's mother.

CHIMENE: . . . Jus' cause you give birth it don't make you a mama.

SHARONDA: It's not like junkies ain't welcome in this house . . .

QUAN enters the kitchen.

CHIMENE *(SHARPLY)*: It's not the same.

OMAR comes back downstairs. He sees QUAN.

OMAR: Mommy says you got two hamsters. Ain't we got enough rodents 'round here?

QUAN: Hamsters know their names, Omar. I'm teachin' Sam and Dave now . . .

OMAR: Sam and Dave? They got names? You a trip little bro . . . you still datin' that Spanish girl?

QUAN: Yeah, we goin' to Lucky Strikes tomorrow night.

OMAR: Trust you to find the one girl in the hood that bowls.

QUAN: I'm savin' up to buy her a pair of Dexter Kerrie bowling shoes for her birthday.

OMAR: Look at you little Romeo . . . how romantic . . . an' how much that gonna cost you, genius?

QUAN: Sixty dollars.

OMAR: Damn little bro, where you gonna get that kind of

money? An' now you got two hamsters to feed . . .

QUAN: I'm baggin' at Food Town. I got $32.45 saved up. I keep it in a jar in my closet.

OMAR: You better hope Daddy don't find it.

QUAN: I hide it under the hamster food. Daddy hates Sam and Dave . . . says they stink up the place.

OMAR: There ain't much Daddy don't hate.

CHIMENE: Now Omar, you come late and I don't want the food to get cold . . . sit down.

OMAR reaches for his fork, and CHIMENE gives him a sharp look. He puts the fork down.

CHIMENE: Lord, thank you for this food that we are about to receive. Thank you for watching over us and keepin' us safe. In the name of Christ Jesus we pray. Amen . . . Omar, we hardly see you for dinner. Who's cookin' for you? I know you not cookin' for yerself.

OMAR: I got a Chinese family cookin' for me. I eat mostly at Wang's Dynasty.

SHARONDA: You got a Black family here an' Wang's cost money.

CHIMENE: Don't start with that Sharonda.

OMAR: You losin' weight, Ma?

CHIMENE: It's the medicine. I can't hold nothin' down.

CHIMENE: Quan chopped those yams so thick. You got to let your mama show you how to slice 'em thin.

SHARONDA: Yeah, I can hardly swallow 'em.

SHARONDA pretends to choke.

QUAN: I put my love in 'em.

SHARONDA: Yeah, yer love stuck in my throat. I hope you don't love dem yams like dat bird you found when you was 'bout six? You loved it fer what? One week?

CHIMENE: What was da name of dat bird?

QUAN: Tweety.

CHIMENE: I wished I known you wasn't feedin' it. Poor thing . . .

OMAR: 'Member da day he brought that mangy street dog home?

CHIMENE: Oh Lord. An' let dat dirty thing up on my sofa. Took me two weeks to get the smell outa da house. An' he smelled as bad as dat dog by the time I got dat creature outta here.

OMAR, CHIMENE, and SHARONDA begin chuckling.

QUAN: Y'all styling. Wasn't dat bad. An' I keep Sam and Dave clean.

SHARONDA: You also let 'em out of the cage to run around the room soon as you got 'em.

QUAN: It ain't right to keep 'em all locked up.

SHARONDA: We chased 'em all over the house.

OMAR: This a good dinner, Ma.

SHARONDA: Neither of you gonna ever find no woman take care of you like Mama. So, you better learn to do fer yerself, 'cause you don't learn how to cook, you ain't gonna eat. Omar, I know you ain't doin' no cookin'.

OMAR: I cook better than you.

SHARONDA: I don't see you complainin' 'bout my mac and cheese. You know I can cook.

QUAN: This from the girl done nearly burned the house down makin' french toast.

SHARONDA: That Teflon pan was no good.

All laugh. On the kitchen table are stacks of photographs.

OMAR: What's all those pictures doin' on the table, Ma?

CHIMENE: I'm makin' albums for you all for when I'm gone. *(She holds up a photo.)* Remember this?

OMAR: No. . .

CHIMENE: That was back home. You was 'bout four. You was always so serious . . . had an old soul.

OMAR: Yeah.

CHIMENE: Look here. This is you and Quan when he was jus' two. That's when we moved here. An' this is Sharonda on that red bicycle. An this is you holdin' Zaire the day he was born. *(She stops, lost in thought.)* I wanted so much for you all.

OMAR: Now Ma . . . don't be worrin' 'bout us.

CHIMENE: Who's goin' to the church with me? None of you children been since yer grandma's passed.

OMAR: Grandma, she live fer Jesus. "All I know is the truth . . ."

OMAR, CHIMENE, SHARONDA, AND QUAN UNISON: . . . "Before I lie to you, I'll say bye to you!"

CHIMENE: She was a Christian woman. She always tryin' to beat the black off yer uncle Robert.

OMAR: That wouldn't be hard, yella as Uncle Robert was.

SHARONDA: That's why he so yella. He used to be black as Daddy.

The door to the apartment opens. Everyone falls silent. JIMMY enters, wearing a black leather jacket and a black leather applejack hat. He walks to the closet, looking in.

CHIMENE: Jimmy, honey, you gonna eat now?

JIMMY: Ain't hungry, Chimene.

CHIMENE: When you gonna eat?

JIMMY: I got to run. I be back.

He takes something from the closet, gives CHIMENE a quick kiss, and leaves.

SHARONDA: I don't know why you keep askin' him to come and eat. You know he ain't gonna eat with us.

CHIMENE: You show respect fer yer father.

SHARONDA: He ain't never home.

CHIMENE: Honor thy father and thy mother, little girl, so that yer days may be long.

OMAR: It say anything in the Bible about him honoring us?

CHIMENE: I know he ain't perfect, but he is still yer father. An' he loves you. In his own way.

Act I, Scene III
JIMMY TRIES

Afternoon. The street. OMAR, clearly unhappy, enters, followed by a junkie.

JUNKIE: Say Omar, can I get two twenties for thirty-five?

OMAR looks at him with disgust.

JUNKIE: Ah, come on Omar. I'm good for it.

OMAR: You have forty dollars or you don't.

JUNKIE: That's hard Omar. I always come to you . . .

OMAR: Yeah, an' you always short.

JUNKIE hands OMAR two twenties.

OMAR: Why you make me treat you like dat? Go down the block and see Quan in the hallway.

JUNKIE exits.

OMAR (*MUTTERING*): Damn uncs walk all over you if you let 'em.

JIMMY enters. When JIMMY speaks he incorporates verbal junk that indicates that the conversation is difficult with his son. He intersperses his talk with long drawn out aaaas, yeahs, slow breathing and low mutterings.

JIMMY: Hey.

Beat.

JIMMY: You know yer mama don't want Quan on the streets.

OMAR: Shorty's in the county fer a few days. I can't do this by myself. I ain't gonna have him out here long.

JIMMY: Mmm-hmn . . . But get him off the streets. He ain't made for the game. What Shorty do to get himself locked up?

OMAR: Boosting . . .

JIMMY: What that nigga try and steal?

OMAR: Underwear.

JIMMY: That boy locked up for a pair of Fruit of the Looms?

OMAR: Yeah.

JIMMY: I don't know why niggas even try to steal. We ain't no good at it. Grab a box of Pampers and we head straight to jail. Now white people, they the Olympians of stealing. Can't compete with white folks when it comes to takin' shit. They wrote the book. Stole the whole damn country.

Beat.

JIMMY: You goin' home?

OMAR: Yeah. I got to give Mommy something fer the rent.

JIMMY glares at OMAR.

JIMMY: Ahhh . . . yer boy's growin' up. Hard to believe he's almost three. He look jus' like you. You still workin' ain't ya?

OMAR: Naw. I lost that job.

JIMMY: Yeah . . . but you got ta find a job. The man see you out here all day no tellin' what he may think.

Beat.

JIMMY: . . . You look like you doin' ok.

OMAR doesn't respond.

JIMMY: . . . Stay smooth . . .

Beat. JIMMY awkwardly lingers, wanting something but unwilling to ask for it. JIMMY starts to go. OMAR, reading his father, reaches into his pants pocket and pulls out a pair of dice.

OMAR: Pop . . .

JIMMY turns back to see OMAR holding a set of dice, an offering. JIMMY cautiously takes the dice and looks at them.

JIMMY: I used to get these in New York . . . have a guy make 'em . . . can't get a pair of 6-8 flats like these no more. Where you git 'em?

OMAR: I caught Wizard cheatin' . . . so he gave 'em to me . . . Ain't no one gonna bet with 'im no more anyway . . . don't nobody trust 'im . . . Said he was jus' gonna bet on me whenever I put 'em down.

JIMMY (*SHAKING THE DICE IN HIS HAND*): Aaahhh, I can start a game with these at the gambling joint right now.

Beat.

OMAR (*CONSIDERING*): a'ight, I git 'em when I come by the house (*JIMMY starts to go*). Pops, you seen Mama's broach, the one she got from grandma?

JIMMY: Why you askin' me that?

OMAR: I'm jus' askin' . . . she been tearin' the house up lookin' for it.

JIMMY gives OMAR a sharp look and walks away. Lights down.

Act I, Scene IV

FAITH

_____

9 a.m.

CHIMENE: Sharonda!

SHARONDA: Huh?

CHIMENE: Come help me zip up this dress . . . an' hurry . . .
Sister Odell be here any minute.

SHARONDA makes her way upstairs

SHARONDA: You look tired, Ma. Maybe you should stay home.
Alex can take me shopping.

CHIMENE: Child, you don't need that boy to take you to no
grocery store. I don't know what he comes sniffing around
here for anyway. Guys give you something they want
something.

SHARONDA: Ain't nobody in this house givin' nobody nothing.
We should have our own car anyway, not be askin'
everyone for rides.

CHIMENE (*CUTTING SHARONDA OFF*): That ol' Buick we had
jus' ate money. Spent more time getting fixed than on the
road . . .

SHARONDA: We still don't got no money, an' we got no car.
How we gonna get all the groceries?

CHIMENE: I'm gonna borrow a few dollars from Sister
Odell . . . everything be fine . . . Now you gonna sit here
complain 'bout what you ain't got? Or is you gonna get

dressed and come with me to church?

SHARONDA: I'm all dressed.

CHIMENE: You ain't all dressed child. You got no slip on.

SHARONDA (*SASHAYING PLAYFULLY*)**:** Never know, I might find me a *fine, fine* God-fearing man in the church. An' he might have a *fine, fine* Cadillac.

CHIMENE: No God-fearing man goin' out with a girl that don't wear a slip. I tell you that.

SHARONDA quickly removes her dress and puts on a slip.

SHARONDA: He better be cute too if I go to all this trouble.

CHIMENE: You put those boys outta yer head and start thinkin' 'bout Jesus. You get yerself right with the Lord and He be right with you. You either in the Word or you ain't little girl. No halfways with the Lord. Holiness ain't no joke.

SHARONDA: How long you know Sister Odell?

CHIMENE: 'Bout thirty years I guess. We worked behind the counter at the diner on East Union when we first come to Newark. When we started wasn't no fun servin' white folks.

SHARONDA: I don't know how you kept yer temper.

CHIMENE: Got one mind for white folks to see, another for what I know is me.

SHARONDA: The Lord at least blessed us with Sister Odell.

CHIMENE: She been a true friend all these years.

CHIMENE (*STARTS TO SING*)**:**

> Walk in the light (walk in the light)
> Beautiful light (well it's a beautiful light)

Come where the dew drops of mercy shine bright (Oh
Lord)
Shine all around us by day and by night
Oh oh oh oh, Jesus is the light of the world . . .

A horn honks from the street.

CHIMENE: That's Sister Odell. Hand me my purse. An' don't
be making eyes at no fellas in church . . .

SHARONDA: Why you think I go to church, Mama?

CHIMENE: You be the death of me Sharonda . . .

They exit the house.

THINGS FALL APART

Afternoon. JIMMY is getting a glass of water in the kitchen. OMAR enters.

OMAR: Hey

JIMMY: Heyyy . . . uuuuh, you seen ya momma?

OMAR: Her and Sharonda was suppose to be going to church. Then Sister Odell takin' 'em to Food Town on the way home.

JIMMY: Boy I tell ya . . . ya momma spend mo' time down at that church than the law allow . . . ain't nobody cook round here, three four dishes in the sank, and they sitting up in a church . . .

OMAR (*INTERRUPTING*): Did you start a game with them dice?

JIMMY: Huh? Oh yeah, I went down to that Puerto Rican gamblin' joint. . . . Them niggas ain't know nothing 'bout no trick dice.

OMAR: You hit em?

JIMMY: Hell yeah. I ain't stop throwing them dice till I turn every last one of they pockets to rabbit ears! Boy I lit their ass up like downtown Atlanta!

OMAR: That's crazy.

JIMMY: Ummmm huh. That's why Wizard like ta go down on that corner and play ya'll . . . he know he can't set them dice down in no real gamblin' joint.

OMAR: Naw?

JIMMY and OMAR sit at the table.

JIMMY: Hell naw!

OMAR: You an' Wizard tight back in the day. . .

JIMMY: Wizard?

OMAR: Wizard say he was the man back then!

JIMMY (*LAUGHS*): That nigga parkin' cars when we come up . . . It was me . . . uhh Cadillac! and . . . Hard Nose! We was the only somebodies knew where to get them dice . . . an' Wizard watched us till we decide to give him a shot.

OMAR: Aw, man.

JIMMY: That nigga ain't know his ass from a hole in da ground! The first time I let him in on the game he fucked up . . . I told him to stay on the dice case da nigga I was gamblin' 'ginst try ta grab' em . . .

OMAR: Why?

JIMMY: That's what they use to do if they thought you was cheating . . . they snatch 'em off the ground and say I caught these. Anyway, I'm tearing this nigga's ass up but I'm making sure the dice hit off the wall and role towards Wizard. Wizard standin' straight up like a goddamn giraffe and he let that nigga reach down and grab my dice!

OMAR: Awe man! What happen!!

JIMMY: Dat nigga took one look at them dice and realized I had him in a trick bag an' we got ta fighting right there. He throwing shit. I'm throwing shit. We tore that gamblin' joint up! When I come up out of there my suede shirt was ripped. I was bleeding on my right side . . . Wizard cross the street holla'in, Jimmy I think that nigga stabbed you!!

OMAR: Wizard ain't help?

JIMMY: Hell no. Took off like a scalded dog. I lost HALF a pint of blood messin' wit that nigga and that other fool that cut me got way wit' my dice. You had ta know what you was doing back then cause a nigga ain't have no problem putting no cold steel in ya ass!

OMAR: Yea.

JIMMY gets up from the table.

JIMMY: Come here. Let me show you how we use ta switch the dice.

OMAR walks over to learn something from his father. JIMMY takes a few bills from his pocket and two sets of red dice.

JIMMY: Ok. I'll teach ya. You need two sets of the same color dice. You keep one set in ya hand wit' the money and the other set in ya shooting hand. Now when you get ready ta switch you reach down and grab the dice with the hand were ya money at. Come on let me show ya.

OMAR and JIMMY kneel on the floor. CHIMENE and SHARONDA walk in.

CHIMENE: What y'all doing?

JIMMY (*CHUCKLING***):** Prayin'

CHIMENE: With dice in ya hand? Y'all go down and get the groceries out of Sister Odell's car.

OMAR (*ATTEMPTING TO KISS CHIMENE ON THE CHEEK WHO MOVES AWAY***):** Hey ma.

CHIMENE: Boy go 'head. You done got just as bad as ya daddy. Where's Quan?

Sharonda: Where he's always at. That bowlin' alley.

Chimene: I'm goin' lay down for a while.

Jimmy and Omar reappear with two bags of groceries.

Jimmy: Where yer mama?

Sharonda: She restin'.

Jimmy: She ate?

Sharonda: She wasn't hungry.

Jimmy: Omar, go get ya momma some of that chicken from that place she like on the corner.

Sharonda: We don't got money for chicken. We short this month on the rent. Mr. Habeeb been here twice this week lookin' to get paid.

Jimmy: We got to feed yer momma before we feed Mr. Habib. *(To Omar)* Hurry up and bring it so she can eat.

Omar: I be back in a minute.

Omar leaves. Sharonda unpacks food while Jimmy checks on Chimene in their bedroom. He takes his hat off and places it on the dresser.

Jimmy: Heeey.

Chimene: Hey.

Jimmy: How you feel?

Chimene: I'm ok . . . a little tired.

Jimmy: I told that boy to brang you some of that chicken from that place you like.

Chimene: I'm not hungry, Jimmy.

Jimmy: You got to eat Chimene . . . got to keep up yer strength. I can cut it up and make you chicken soup. I'll put the lemon juice and red pepper flakes in it. You like that.

CHIMENE: I try . . . they locked that boy up from cross the street.

JIMMY: He was out there everyday like the man don't know what he doing.

CHIMENE: He ain't doing nothing but what he saw everybody else do.

JIMMY: You hear 'bout that boy got shot?

CHIMENE: Kareem Johnson?

JIMMY: Yeah, Quan's friend.

CHIMENE: Boys always getting shot. I know his mama.

OMAR returns and finds SHARONDA putting away groceries.

OMAR: Where Mommy?

SHARONDA: She wit' Daddy. You get that chicken?

OMAR: Yeah.

JIMMY (*YELLING*): That Omar?

SHARONDA: Yeah!

JIMMY: Bring ya momma that food.

OMAR hands her the bag of food. Stops himself.

OMAR: Wait, let me take out some wings for Zaire.

He takes out two wings.

SHARONDA: I don't think mommy be eatin' much . . . an' I don't think she should be eatin' fried chicken . . .

JIMMY: Uhhhh Brang me two plates! (*SHARONDA begins to grab two plates.*) You took ya medicine?

CHIMENE: No, not yet.

JIMMY: Sharonda!

SHARONDA: Huh?

JIMMY: Brang ya momma some water so she can take her medicine!

SHARONDA leaves the plates and food and quickly brings the glass of water to JIMMY.

JIMMY (*TO SHARONDA*): Where the food?

SHARONDA: Omar bringin' it.

JIMMY takes the glass from SHARONDA and hands it to CHIMENE along with two pills that he takes from a pill bottle on the dresser. CHIMENE sits up in the bed and takes the pills and hands the glass back to JIMMY who places it on the dresser.

JIMMY: Tell that boy to hurry up wit' your momma's food.

SHARONDA moves downstairs. JIMMY sits on the bed and gently rubs CHIMENE's shoulders. Lights dim on CHIMENE and JIMMY.

SHARONDA (*TO OMAR*): That man up there 'bout to drive me crazy.

OMAR: He'll be alright.

OMAR: You do that alcoholism prevention class they made you take?

SHARONDA: Yeah. An' they charged me three hundred and forty dollars.

OMAR: An' you see that therapist like the court wanted?

SHARONDA: Yeah. An' they charged me one hundred and fifty dollars for that.

OMAR: An' you do your community service?

SHARONDA: Omar . . .

OMAR: Sharonda . . .

SHARONDA: Yeah. I washed city garbage trucks for a day.

OMAR: You payin' your fines?

SHARONDA: It ain't like we got a car to drive . . .

OMAR: I'm jus' askin'. You payin' your fines?

OMAR (*SHARPLY*)**:** Sharonda . . .

SHARONDA: They a hundred and fifty dollars a month. Where I gonna get that kind of money? I jus' gave 'em four hundred and ninety dollars an' I had to borrow most of that from you and Sadiye . . .

OMAR: You don't pay it they come lookin' for ya. I don't know why you was drivin' Sadiye's car for anyway?

SHARONDA: 'Cause she was drunk.

OMAR: Like you wasn't drunk?

SHARONDA: My blood alcohol level was .05. The legal limit is .08. I wasn't drunk . . .

OMAR: You drunk enough to spend a night in the country . . .

SHARONDA: You lecturing me 'bout drinkin'?

Lights dim on OMAR and SHARONDA. Lights rise on CHIMENE and JIMMY.

JIMMY: You get all yer medicine this week?

CHIMENE: Most of it.

JIMMY: You know Omar's runnin' the streets again.

CHIMENE: He in the streets 'cause you in the streets.

JIMMY: What I got to do with him runnin' the streets?

CHIMENE: He jus' like you, Jimmy. He got a hard head.

Pause.

We used to have family day on Sunday . . . Coney

Island . . . Asbury Park . . .

JIMMY: They don't remember that.

CHIMENE: Omar and Sharonda remember. But Quan never had that. That boy terrified of you. That's why he distant.

JIMMY: That boy soft. That have nothin' to do with me.

CHIMENE: An' Omar, I'm afraid of losing him for good this time. He the only one holdin' this family together. He get locked up we got nothin'.

JIMMY (*ANGRY*): Now he the man around here?

CHIMENE: He payin' the bills . . .

JIMMY (*GLOWERING*): You can't tell dat boy nothin'. I seen 'im the other day on the corner. I told him 'bout being out there.

CHIMENE: An' what was you doin' out der?

JIMMY: What that got to do with me talkin' to him on the corner? I told him 'bout being out there. You tryin' to make it 'bout me.

CHIMENE: Why not? Ain't none of us blind, Jimmy . . . out der gettin' high . . . runnin' the streets. An' these kids done followed you right out the door. Next thing you know Omar be locked up.

JIMMY: Ain't nobody followin' me out no door.

CHIMENE: You believe that?

JIMMY: I worked any job I could get when we come up here. I picked vegetables like a field nigga. I cleaned toilets in the bus station. I worked overnights in that warehouse. I was puttin' in seventy hours a week, an' we still poor.

CHIMENE (*SPEAKING OVER JIMMY*): I'm talking about now.

Now, Jimmy. That was then!

JIMMY (*YELLING*): Omar!

OMAR: What?

JIMMY: What'chu talking about, "What?" Where's the damn food?

OMAR: This nigga.

SHARONDA takes the food. She carries two plates with food upstairs to JIMMY and CHIMENE. The sight/smell of the food make CHIMENE queasy. SHARONDA and JIMMY notice without commentary. SHARONDA leaves.

CHIMENE: We was a family Jimmy. We had Omar and Sharonda in that good white school. We wasn't livin' in the ghetto. We getting' by. They wasn't turning off the gas and the electric. Food money wasn't disappearing, along with jus' about anything else in this house, to feed your habit. If you'd stayed in church . . .

JIMMY: You been shouting, clapping, and screaming hallelujahs for years an' nothin's changed. I figured we done give God long enough.

CHIMENE: That's the dope talkin'. Jesus stand with the crucified. The last is first the first last.

JIMMY: Try livin' by that in the streets. You built yerself a whole world to live in but it ain't the real one, Chimene.

CHIMENE: Those streets evil and that evil in my house. I fightin' Satan best I know how.

JIMMY: . . . Thanking the Lord for turkey cold cuts on Thanksgiving . . .

CHIMENE: We had each other. We sit down as a family. It

don't matter what was on the plate. Can't you see that? Or you gonna wait to figure that out when I'm gone?

Lights rise on OMAR and SHARONDA. OMAR searches in the closet for something he is unable to find. He approaches SHARONDA.

OMAR (*TO SHARONDA*): Did you move my stuff?

SHARONDA: What stuff?

OMAR: Sharonda . . .

SHARONDA: I don't know what you're talking about.

OMAR: Sharonda, I'm not in the moo . . .

SHARONDA (*INTERRUPTING*): Ain't nobody touch nothin' of yours!

OMAR goes back for a second look. JIMMY appears. OMAR glares at JIMMY.

OMAR: Did you move my stuff?

JIMMY: Nigga don't be RUNNING UP asking me no damn questions.

OMAR: Did you move my stuff?

JIMMY: What you mean did I move ya stuff! What stuff?

OMAR: Don't act like you don't know what the fuck I'm talking about.

JIMMY: I know good and hell well you ain't bring no drugs in this house!

OMAR: All I want to know is did you touch my stuff?

JIMMY: Stay right there. I got ya stuff.

JIMMY turns and walks away. OMAR heads back into the bedroom. CHIMENE hears the commotion and comes out of the room. She finds JIMMY mumbling angrily while going through the hall closet.

CHIMENE: Jimmy, what's going on?

SHARONDA (*FROM DOWNSTAIRS*): Daddy?

JIMMY (*MUMBLING TO HIMSELF*): Wait right there. I got your stuff.

CHIMENE: Jimmy?

JIMMY: Stay out of this!

CHIMENE leaves and goes in the hallway to talk to OMAR.

CHIMENE: What's going on with you and ya daddy?

OMAR: Nothin'.

CHIMENE: He in that hall closet lookin' for something.

OMAR: Oh, it's like that.

OMAR takes out his gun and waits for JIMMY. He makes sure CHIMENE doesn't see the weapon.

CHIMENE: Stay here let me go talk to him.

JIMMY enters with his shotgun wrapped in a towel.

CHIMENE: Jimmy.

OMAR: What's up?

JIMMY: Nigga don't say shit to me an' I won't say shit to you!

OMAR: Youz a washed-up junkie. You steal anything you get ya hands on!

CHIMENE (*RAISING HER VOICE*): Omar!

SHARONDA (*HYSTERICAL*): Walk away, Omar. Just walk away.

JIMMY: Nigga, if you don't get the hell out of here I swear I'm gone blow ya damn head off!

OMAR pulls out his pistol.

CHIMENE (*COMMANDING*): Omar, GO!

JIMMY: Oh, you a big man now. Shoot, nigga!

CHIMENE (*GRABBING JIMMY*): Jimmy, NO!

SHARONDA (*PUSHING OMAR TOWARD THE DOOR*): Omar, go!

OMAR: You lucky you in Mommy's house . . .

> *OMAR and JIMMY stare at each other as OMAR backs out the door. OMAR tucks the gun back into his belt under his shirt. JIMMY turns to CHIMENE.*

JIMMY: Where's Jesus now, Chimene?

AFTERMATH

———

Projection: ZAIRE at five.

NIGHT. SOUND MONTAGE: *Gun shots, tires screeching, car doors slamming, police sirens/cops shouting: "Don't fucking move, get down!*

OFFICER 1: We got a half dozen people saw you and Malik in a fight. Next thing, we get a call 'cause his body is in back of a warehouse.

OMAR (*TO AUDIENCE*): Projects like jail . . .

OFFICER 1: Be smart, Omar. Give us a statement. Help yourself.

OMAR: Mess hall jus' like the school cafeteria . . .

OFFICER 2: We aren't going to give you a chance later.

OMAR: Yard like the playground . . .

OFFICER 1: You sure you don't have nothing to say?

OMAR: Metal detectors . . .

OFFICER 2: Take him back to the holding cell.

OMAR: Cops . . .

Enter ADDICT from earlier scene.

OFFICER 1: Omar gonna walk if you don't help us, an' we know he did it. Help us on this one or you goin' back inside. An' you don't want to be dope sick all weekend in the County, do ya?

OMAR: The rules flip . . .

OFFICER 2: This time the judge might keep you.

OMAR: Loyalties crumble . . .

ADDICT: I'll sign it. But you got to give me more than a hundred dollars. This one ain't right. It ain't right . . .

OMAR: Prison ain't no culture shock. Been conditioned my whole life for this . . .

THE SCORE, OR THE NEW DEAL

Morning. In the visiting room of the Green Street Essex
County Jail. QUAN walks to the booth and forces a smile.

OMAR: What's up, Lil Bro?

QUAN: What's up? You puttin' on weight.

OMAR: You know the shit.

OMAR flexes his muscles for QUAN.

QUAN: Yo, you gonna cop out?

OMAR: How Sharonda doin'?

QUAN: She messin' with that Latin King nigga from Newark
whose man in there with you.

OMAR: What she doin' with him?

QUAN: I don't know, but he helpin' a little with the rent.

OMAR: Tell Sharonda stay away from that Latin King dude.
That nigga known all over Newark.

QUAN: Sharonda gonna do what she do . . .

OMAR: Tell her I said don't see that nigga.

OFFICER (*SHOUTING*): Visits will be over in two minutes! Not
three, not four, two minutes! If you're not out of the booth
in two minutes you won't get a visit next week!

Beat.

QUAN (*LOOKING ANGRILY TOWARD CORRECTIONS OFFICER*): I
jus' got in here . . . Omar, you gonna cop out or what?

Pause.

OMAR: They'll drop the kidnapping, if I cop out to second degree reckless.

QUAN: Kidnapping? You ain't kidnap nobody!

OMAR: It's a BS charge. They cleaned up a few junkies and have 'em as witnessesses . . . 'an then it's the cop's word 'gainst yours. Can't beat that. It's the ol' trick. I get thirty or I plea out they give me seventeen . . .

QUAN: Seventeen! That's hard, Omar. You gonna tell Mommy?

OMAR nods.

OFFICER: Let's go!

OMAR: Get that money from Shorty and take care of Mommy's medicine. I call you next week.

QUAN nods, hangs up and walks out the visiting hall. He passes CHIMENE but averts his eyes.

CHIMENE: Hey, son, how's your spirit?

OMAR: It's holding, Mommy.

CHIMENE: Did you get the scriptures I sent?

OMAR: Naw, I ain't get 'em. (*OMAR laughs.*)

CHIMENE: Ummmmhuh . . . Make sure you share them with the fellas in there.

OMAR: Ma . . . These guys don't read no scriptures.

CHIMENE (*PLAYFULLY*): Well, you be sure and read some to them, knoowaan I'm saying . . .

OMAR: Yeah, I know . . . How you feeling?

OFFICER: Keep ya hands off the glass! Visit's over in ten minutes!

OMAR: We just sat down!

CHIMENE: Omar, that man ain't bothering us. I'm feeling fine. I was thinking about taking a trip to Georgia.

OMAR: Daddy going?

CHIMENE: He need to go. He's been running them streets a lot more since you got locked up . . . he's not taking you being in here too well . . .

OMAR: He ain't worried about me being in here.

CHIMENE: Ya father loves all y'all. He don't know what it's like to have a father-son relationship. Your grandfather was a hard man. He raised ya father to be hard. Daddy was a good worker when he first come up North. He didn't know nothing about no drugs.

OMAR: Didn't take him long to figure it out.

Pause.

OMAR: I'm jus' saying, Ma, at the end of the day he didn't do nothing for nobody!

CHIMENE: You don't remember ya father taking us to Coney Island?

OMAR: I remember him getting high and us being hungry. I remember warming my hand in front of the stove cause the heat was off! I remember putting the food on the back porch to keep it cold 'cause the electricity was out and we in the dark.

CHIMENE: Your father wanted . . .

OMAR: Ma you been making excuses for him my whole life! He ain't do nothing for us! I walked to school with holes in my shoes and my coat! I used to hate the sunlight 'cause I couldn't hide the stains.

CHIMENE: We was together!

OMAR: We'd been better off without him . . .

CHIMENE: Omar!

OFFICER: Visits are over in five minutes!

OMAR: He wasn't there, Ma.

CHIMENE: I was there! I was right there with y'all and do you think it was easy for me?

OMAR: He took our childhood.

CHIMENE: Now you takin' Zaire's.

OMAR: Yeah, but ain't nobody making excuses for me. I'm not making excuses for myself.

CHIMENE: Jimmy didn't have no education like you. He broke himself working all those night jobs before he started selling dope . . . hangin' out in bars, gambling joints, pool halls . . . hustling . . . trying to provide. Same as you.

OFFICER: Okay. Time's up!

CHIMENE: You're not so different you and your daddy. That's all I'm tryna say. Let me get out of here so you don't get in no trouble.

OMAR: Ain't nobody paying no attention to that clown, Ma.

CHIMENE: Do what you suppose to do . . . I can see you next week.

OMAR (*STANDING UP*): Ma, I had to take a plea.

CHIMENE: You ain't going to trial?

OMAR: They stacked too many charges, Ma. If I go to trial I get thirty. They willin' to cut it to seventeen if I cop.

CHIMENE looks perplexed. Pause.

OMAR: Ones who go to trial get the longest sentences.

CHIMENE: That's a long time, Omar. You didn't do it. An' the family . . .

OMAR: I know, Ma. I know. Bring Zaire next time you come.

OFFICER: Let's go!

CHIMENE (*VISIBLY SHAKEN*): I sent you a few dollars so you can get some things. I be back with Zaire next week. I love you, son.

OMAR: I love you too, Ma.

The two hang up their phones and force a smile for the other. With eyes locked, they wave.

THE SYSTEM

Projection: ZAIRE at seven.

Morning. Scarborough Prison in Trenton, New Jersey.
Prisoners are brought in, shackled hand and foot to five to
ten other prisoners. The room is noisy. OFFICER WATKINS,
a large Black man, stands in front of the prisoners.
WATKINS addresses OMAR and the other inmates.

WATKINS: My name is Officer Watkins. This is Officer
Watkins's prison. What Officer Watkins say in Officer
Watkins's prison goes. Officer Watkins don't care why
you here. Officer Watkins don't care who you are. Officer
Watkins sure don't care who you think you are. As long as
you here you do what Officer Watkins say. Is that clear?

Pause.

WATKINS: Are you motherfuckers deaf? Officer Watkins said,
"Is that clear?"

PRISONERS (_IN UNISON_): Yes!

WATKINS: When Officer Watkins call you up to the bench
you step up. You state your full name and date of birth.
Are we clear?

PRISONERS (_IN UNISON_): Yes!

WATKINS: If you fail to comply with Officer Watkins's
instructions, we will drag your sorry ass to the hole. An'
you can stay down there for six months, an' we can try this

again. Is that clear?

PRISONERS (*IN UNISON*): Yes!

WATKINS: First man in line. Step up and state your name and date of birth.

OMAR: Omar Moore. August 17, 1975.

OMAR complies with this and all of WATKINS's instructions. As OMAR strips the lights slowly close in on him so that by the time he is naked he is alone in the spotlight surrounded by darkness.

WATKINS: Take off your coat and hat. Drop it on the floor. Hand Officer Watkins your shirt. Slowly take off your T-shirt and hand it to Officer Watkins. Hand Officer Watkins your boots. Bang 'em together and hand 'em to me. Take off your socks. Turn 'em inside out. Hand 'em to me. Don't shake 'em. Take off your pants. Hand 'em to me. Take off your boxers. Turn 'em inside out. Drop 'em. Stretch out your arms. Let me see your palms. Are you wearing dentures?

OMAR: No.

WATKINS: Open your mouth wide. Stick out your tongue. Lift up your top lip. Pull your bottom lip down. Lift your arms straight in the air so I can see your armpits. Bend your right ear. Bend your left ear. Fingers through your hair. Lift your piece. Lift your nut sack. Turn around. Lift your right foot. Lift your left foot. Bend over. Spread your cheeks. Cough. Ok. Get dressed. Walk to the end of the hallway. Face the wall. Don't say shit.

Lights go down.

UNDERGROUND

Morning. OMAR walks to the phones as another prisoner,
BLOOD MONEY, reaches the phone at the same time.

BLOOD MONEY (*SNATCHING THE PHONE*): I'm using this,
nigga.

OMAR says nothing and moves to the other phone.

BLOOD MONEY: I'm using that one too, nigga.

OMAR: So, what you saying?

BLOOD MONEY (*GETTING IN OMAR'S FACE*): I'm saying Blood
rule up here . . . Get down or lay down nigga. Either you
gonna be blood or you gonna bleed. You pick up that
phone I slice you a buck fifty from your ear to your thick
ass lips.

OMAR: Yo, I ain't come here for no trouble my man . . . jus'
tryin' to fight my case.

BLOOD MONEY: You know what it is . . . you gotta roll.

OMAR: I ain't goin' nowhere, fam.

BLOOD MONEY: I ain't ya fuckin' fam!

OMAR: Yo, I don't even know you, bruh.

BLOOD MONEY: My name BLOOD MONEY, nigga! This is my
tier! I run this shit! Niggas do what I say or get poked the
fuck up!

ALAMEEN, AN OLDER PRISONER: Come on, young brothers,
we all in here fightin' the crackers. We can't be in here

fightin' each other. Ya'll let that go.

OMAR looks at BLOOD MONEY. OMAR and BLOOD MONEY stare at each other for a few seconds. Then OMAR picks up the phone. He begins to dial a number while BLOOD MONEY looks intently at him.

OMAR: Hey. How's Mommy doin'? You think ya'll gonna be able to make it up here this weekend? If you get a ride, bring Zaire . . .

Act I, Scene X

INITIATION

_____

Afternoon.

VOICES: Movie up! Yo, MD! You goin' out? Shower on four tier.

The sound of a cell door opening electronically. OJORE enters the cell. The sound of door closing.

OJORE: What's yer name, young 'un?

OMAR: Omar.

OJORE: County or prison?

OMAR (*APPREHENSIVELY*): CRAF.

OJORE: Where you from?

OMAR: Newark.

OJORE: Me too. This your first time down?

OMAR: Yeah, this shit is crazy.

OJORE: Yeah, but you be a'ight. Go 'head, toss your stuff up on the bunk. That's you up there. You don't got much right now, but when you get situated those shelves over there and that locker at the foot of the bed are yours. Want a soda?

OMAR (*HESITANTLY—HE HAS BEEN WARNED NOT TO TAKE ANYTHING FROM ANYONE IN THE PRISON*): Nah, I'm good.

OJORE: Suit ya' self. If you want it later yer welcome to it.

OMAR: 'Preciate that, but I'm good.

OJORE: I ain't on no BS! You got people out there in the world?

OMAR, anxious, says nothing.

OJORE: I'm only asking 'cause it might be a minute before you get a pin number. I'll call my ol' lady later on. I can have her get in touch with your people and let them know where you at.

OMAR: Nah, I'm . . .

OJORE: I know you good. An' I know you jus' coming in. An' I know you probably got all kinda crazy stuff runnin' through ya' head. I jus' tryna help.

OMAR: My bad.

OJORE: I was where you are thirty years ago. Back then all dem crazy thoughts you havin' was my reality.

Pause.

OJORE: If you gonna be in here wit' me we gotta get a few things straight.

OMAR: I'm listening.

OJORE: First, this ain't my cage. It ain't your cage. It belong to the state. Since we gotta be in it we gotta keep it clean. Bugs and mice get crazy in here. One bunky is enough.

OMAR: I feel you.

There is a sudden tap on the door.

SLASH: As-Salamu Alaikim, Ojore. What's happening?

OJORE: Wa Alaikum As-Salaam, Slash. I'll get wit' you in a minute. Let me finish holla'n at my man here.

SLASH: Yo, I come to holla at him real quick tho.

OJORE: About what?

SLASH: Your name Omar Moore?

OMAR looks to OJORE for assurance.

OMAR: Yeah.

SLASH: I'm Slash. Used to run with yer pops. Knew you when you was 'bout this big (*holds up his hand to his waist*). Used to call me Uncle Bip.

OMAR: Yeah, yeah. You and my pop was in heavy. You was like my godfather.

SLASH: I'll get this cop to bust the door so you can get this stuff. Hold on.

SLASH waves to a guard. The electric whine of the locking system as the lock is disengaged. OJORE grabs a candy bar off his shelf and tosses it to SLASH who gives OMAR a large laundry bag, filled with commissary items.

SLASH (*PICKING UP A COPY OF BLACK JACOBINS FROM OJORE'S BUNK*): What you readin' now Ojore . . . Black Jac . . . o . . . bins . . .

OJORE (*OPENS THE BOOK AND READS*): "The cruelties of property and privilege are always more ferocious than the revenges of poverty and oppression. For the one aims at perpetuating resented injustice, the other is merely a momentary passion soon appeased . . ."

SLASH (*TO OMAR*): You in here with yer own professor . . .

OJORE: Black Jacobins . . . C.L.R. James . . . Haitian Revolution . . . only successful slave revolt in human history an' Haiti been payin' for it ever since.

SLASH: I'm holla at cha later. I gotta bounce. As-Salaamu Alaikum, Ojore. Peace Omar, I'll be around.

OJORE: Wa Alaikum As-Salaam, Akhi! I'll git wit ya later.

OMAR dumps the bag onto his bed. Soap, toothpaste, deodorant, shampoo, underclothes, packets of noodle soup, pouched beans, assorted packages of seafood, rice, a Walkman, earbuds, a stinger, and a handwritten note.

OMAR: He ain't have to do all that.

OJORE: Yeah, he did.

OMAR: Whatchu mean?

OJORE: If he yer godfather or whatever, he goin' look out for ya. He got to, out of respect for yer pops. It ain't got nothin' to do with you. Slash from the old school. He live by the old code. Loyalty everything to dudes like Slash.
OJORE walks to his hot-pot.

OJORE: You want something to eat? I got some mack and rice.

OMAR: Mack?

OJORE: Mackerel. Fish. Like salmon, but it ain't.

OMAR: Nah, I'm good.

OJORE: Listen, dey got mystery meat in da mess hall for lunch. you ain't gonna want dat, I promise you. You betta get in on dis while ya can. I ain't gonna ask again.
Pause.

OMAR: A'ight, I'll take some.

OJORE opens his storage bin. He pulls out a new bowl. He fills it with mackerel and rice. He passes it to OMAR along with a new cup and a plastic spoon.

OJORE: You can keep all dat. When you get yerself situated witcha money and all dat, jus' make sure you replace it for the next brotha coming in. We goin' to the yard soon . . .
OJORE begins to ready himself to go out into the yard. He

ties his boots tight. He tucks in his shirt. He forcefully pulls down his hat. OMAR, watching, mimics his preparations.

OMAR: What you do there?

OJORE: I walk. I work the pile. I play some hoops. Now, there are places in the yard you want to stay clear of. 'An when they bust the gate, you gotta move quick. When they close the break you miss out and be locked in.

The gate opens. OJORE and OMAR walk to the yard. The light changes. They each have a more menacing posture.

OJORE: That new cement used to be dirt. Pigs got tired runnin' metal detectors over it 'cuz of so many buried shanks.

OJORE pulls OMAR by the arm over towards him.

OJORE: Those lines for the runners. Can't walk in them. Block a runner you got a problem.

Sounds fill the space. There is a sound indicating large weights being dropped.

OMAR: What's that?

OJORE: Mama Herc.

OMAR: Mama Herc?

OJORE: Mama Hercules . . . He shashay 'round here at night with his Fruit of the Looms all rolled up wigglin' his hips . . . talkin' about boy pussy. That's when you gonna LIKE being locked in a cage . . .

OMAR: Damn . . .

OJORE: He do six hundred-pound dead lifts . . . bar bends . . . He's every new fish's worst nightmare . . . a Black Goliath . . . I seen him lift up a new fish with one hand by the throat and kiss him on the lips . . . Poor kid didn't know what hit 'em . . . an' Mama Herc got breath smell like a dead dog . . . He say 'white boy, I'm gonna suck your dick,' an' he did . . . Then he say, 'now white boy you gonna suck mine' . . . But look, he got a story too . . . they all do . . . state raised . . . raped in juvenile homes . . . never had a mama or a papa . . . grew up . . . got huge . . . started doin' unto others what was done unto him . . . But inside he a scared, little boy . . . can't hardly read or write . . . never had a job . . . never drove a car . . . don't know how to talk to women . . . spent mostly his whole life locked up . . . This the only world he got . . . in here he king of the weight pile . . . he a legend . . . he Mama Herc. The biggest man in da prison in the daytime an' the biggest bitch at night.

RADICAL LOVE (REDUX)

---

3 a.m. The cell. OMAR and OJORE in their bunks. OJORE is asleep. OMAR can hear other prisoners threatening to mess each other up in the yard the next day: "I'm goin' ta sharpen my shit tomorrow morning." "When the doors bust you bust." OMAR sits up, frightened. MR. CHARLIE appears like an apparition in the half-light outside the cell.

MR. CHARLIE (*QUIETLY*): Young'en, what you doin' up?

OMAR climbs down from his upper bunk.

OMAR: Who you?

MR. CHARLIE: Jus' ol' Mr. Charlie . . . let me see yer face?

MR. CHARLIE (*EXAMINES OMAR'S FACE CLOSELY*): What's yer name?

OMAR: Omar Moore.

MR. CHARLIE: Where you from, Omar?

OMAR: Newark.

MR. CHARLIE: You Jimmy Moore's son?

OMAR: Yeah.

MR. CHARLIE: I knew him back in the day. An' I don't know if it is good or bad luck but when he come into Scarborough he was in this very cell. Yer in yer daddy's bed.

Lights dim.

Lights up. Sound of alarm. Then a siren above the alarm. The prison is on lockdown. No one can leave the cells. The intercom, over the alarm and siren: Code sixty-six. Code sixty-six. After several minutes, the code is over. Alarm and siren cease. OMAR, confused, looks up at OJORE in his bunk.

OJORE: Probably a fight . . .

PRISONER (*SHOUTING FROM OFFSTAGE*): Some nigga on 4-Wing hung himself. Shot his appeal down.

OJORE (*SIGHING*): I seen a lot of that.

OMAR: Who's Mr. Charlie?

OJORE: He a ghost. You seen Mr. Charlie?

OMAR: Last night.

OJORE: He's the prison house nigga . . . spits and polishes the boots of the pigs. He's what we all supposed to become. Jus' sent two punks to the hole for a brick of dope . . . but I think ol' Mr. Charlie done snitched once too often . . . Mr. Charlie goin' get his.

Beat.

OMAR: What you in here for, Brother Ojore?

OJORE: Don't be askin' nobody what dey in for. People take stuff like that another way.

Long pause.

OJORE: I expropriated monies in Newark from a capitalist bank . . . got into a gunfight with the political police.

OMAR: Political police?

OJORE: Yeah, all police is political. They serve the system don't they? An' what's that system? Capitalism.

OMAR: That's some heavy shit, Ojore . . .

OJORE: Look son, our bodies ain't worth nothin' to the man on the streets. Once we locked in a cage we worth $50,000 a year to all dem prison contractors, guards, food service companies, phone companies, laundry services, medical companies an' prison construction companies. An' in here we can't create no problems. People say da system don't work. That's 'cause they don't get it. The system works jus' the way it designed to work.

OMAR: What you cop, Ojore?

OJORE: Two life bids.

OMAR: Damn . . .

OJORE: I was arrested with New Afrikan POW Kojo Bomani Sababu and Andaliwa Clark. . . killed in action inside these walls after he shot two pigs in the MCU trying to escape. I got twenty-two years in the MCU . . .

OMAR: Twenty-two years . . .

OJORE: They kept Black revolutionaries from the population . . .

OMAR: Why?

OJORE: Had to break us . . . Couldn't let us preach resistance . . . Had to have someone to refine their torture techniques on . . . Wanted to make sure the rest of you stayed asleep.

OMAR: Whatchu mean, "asleep"?

OJORE: You read George Jackson, Julius Lester?

OMAR: I don't do books.

OJORE: Brother, in this cell we do books. We ain't goin' sit with our mouths half open all day lookin' at Basketball Wives. Take this.

OJORE hands him a book—Malcolm X Speaks

OJORE: Consider this the college you never had. An' when you finish with brother Malcolm X you can read brother George Jackson and start on those law books, 'cause you the only one ever goin' help you get out of here.

Sound of the blues song "Born Under a Bad Sign" being played on a guitar and sung by SHAKY BROWN.

SHAKY BROWN (*SINGING*): Born under a bad sign I been down since I begin to crawl / If it wasn't for bad luck, I wouldn't have no luck at all / Hard luck and trouble is my only friend I been on my own ever since I was ten / Born under a bad sign I been down since I begin to crawl If it wasn't for bad luck, I wouldn't have no luck at all . . .

OMAR: Who's that?

OJORE: Shaky Brown. He playin' for that boy from 4-wing . . . he playin' for all that boy's friends. He playin' 'cause in prison you can't cry, not in public anyway. You can't show grief. This a house of grief. Can't throw any more grief on the brothers here. Got to do your grieving alone . . . when someone's pops or moms is gone, Shaky starts to play. He's our preacher, our undertaker, our pallbearer, our church choir an' our gravedigger.

OMAR: The small dude with the white hair?

OJORE: Almost eighty.

OMAR: Not out?

OJORE: This system shattered Shaky into a million pieces. He state-raised like Mama Herc . . . started in juvenile . . . spent his life more in than out of the prison system. These state-raised can't navigate on the outside. Most of 'em harder than the concrete and steel that encapsulates them in their cages, but inside they broken, need the prison to feel normalcy.

OMAR: That life make you crazy.

OJORE: You got that right son. Most of Shaky's life lived in his head. But I tell you the amazing thing about Shaky is he never done drugs like most of the state raised. He paints. He plays the guitar, self-taught . . . can't read a note . . . strictly by ear . . . only play blues. They have some of his art in the Recreation Department. He paints family for prisoners 'an they hang it in their cells.

OMAR: So, he's gonna die in here?

OJORE: Yeah, an' that's what he wants . . . carried out shackled and chained, 'cause the rules say corpses got to be shackled and chained when they taken out of the prison . . . like we gunna rise up from the dead and make a run for it. He goes before the parole board . . . tells the white board members they crackers and the Black ones they Uncle Toms, tells 'em that they can shove their rehabilitation programs up their ass . . . that he'd still knife that white boy. . . that cracker had it comin' . . . he'll never be sorry for what he did. . . back into the prison he comes . . . Only time that parole board hears the truth.

OMAR: For real?

OJORE: What's Shaky on the outside? Jus' an old Black man . . . no family, no money, no home, no name. Here he's Shaky Brown . . . the man who fights the angel of death.

SHAKY BROWN (*SINGING*): I can't read, haven't learned how to write / My whole life has been one big fight / Born under a bad sign I been down since I begin to crawl / If it wasn't for bad luck, I wouldn't have no luck at all I ain't lyin' / If it wasn't for bad luck I wouldn't have no kind-a luck / If it wasn't for real bad luck, I wouldn't have no luck at all.

INSIDE/OUTSIDE

Projection: ZAIRE at eight.

CHIMENE and JIMMY are in the apartment.

CHIMENE: We got to give Mr. Habeeb something, Jimmy. We three months behind.

JIMMY: He can wait. We don't have much comin' in. Quan got that job baggin but he spendin' all his money on bowlin' and those pet rats . . .

CHIMENE: They hamsters. An' I'm not takin' money from Quan. He got so little in his life as it is, 'specially with Omar gone.

JIMMY: Well, money don't fall from heaven no matter what that preacher tells you Chimene.

CHIMENE: Sister Odell give me something. An' Shorty come by with forty dollars. I give that to Mr. Habeeb. That hold us for a while. Sharonda askin' her boyfriend to help. The good Lord see us through. He always does.

JIMMY: I pick something up at the gamblin' joint. You know my luck.

CHIMENE: Quan and Zaire takin' this awful hard. I want you to talk to 'em. He didn't kill that boy, Jimmy.

JIMMY: Since when that matter?

CHIMENE: If he went to trial the truth come out.

JIMMY: That never happen, Chimene. The system see to

that. The ones go to trial get the longest sentences jus' to remind everyone else they better do jus' what the man tells 'em to do.

CHIMENE: I'm prayin' for him every night. I prayin' we get him home.

JIMMY: Throw in something 'bout the rent. Maybe God give us two miracles. We overdue.

The sound of the front door being opened in the hallway.

CHIMENE: That the mail. See if we got a letter from Omar.

JIMMY leaves. He comes back with a few envelopes.

JIMMY: He write.

JIMMY hands the letter to CHIMENE who opens it. In a spotlight on the other side of the stage OMAR appears. OMAR reads the letter.

OMAR: Mommy, Daddy, Quan, and Sharonda, I'm doin' okay. My bunky is an ol' head, was a big revolutionary back in the day. He watchin' out for me. An' I see Uncle Bib. He make sure I got everything I need. He tryin' to get me a job in the kitchen where he work. I get to work out in the yard. An' I see ol' Mr. Charlie who was in here with you, Pops. He says I in yer old cell. What the odds of that? I know things is tight. I wish I was there to help. Quan, you got to stay home. Try and finish school. Shorty headin' for trouble. Stay away from him. Sharonda, the food so bad in here I miss your cookin', even your burnt french toast. An' Daddy, I sure could use those dice if you could figure out a way to slip 'em in here. Tell Zaire I'll call as soon as I get some money on my phone card. I know the visits hard, but I want to see my boy. I got his pictures, the new ones, over the bunk. He's growin' up. His daddy so proud of him. Mommy, take care of yerself. Don't be worrin' 'bout me. I good as long as you're good. I gave those scripture verses you send to the men in the fellowship group. They appreciate 'em. I miss you all. Love, Omar

QUAN STEPS UP

Afternoon. QUAN and SHORTY on the street.

SHORTY: What's good, man?

QUAN: You get rid of yer car, Shorty?

SHORTY: Yeah, I did . . . that's my new ride.

QUAN: A black Charger?

SHORTY: Yeah.

QUAN: Shorty, man, we in the slums. I'm tryin' to be out here when my brother gets home . . . you tryin' to get us cased up.

SHORTY: What, you're buggin. . .

QUAN: I'm not buggin. You're nineteen. No license. No job. How you payin' for that car? And dog, if the cops start sniffin' round you they be sniffin' round me.

SHORTY: I ain't no snitch, nigga!

QUAN: I know that. I'm jus' saying cops do their homework. They put two and two together. That's us two.

SHORTY: What good is havin' shit if you can't show it?

QUAN: You want to spend your cash, pay your Moms rent or something.

SHORTY: Fuck, man.

Beat.

SHORTY: Yo, when Omar getting out?

QUAN: He got seventeen, but I'm gonna get a lawyer for a sentence reduction. Then I'm out this shit. We goin' into business together . . .

SHORTY: But we in the game, dog.

QUAN: Nah man, this shit for the birds. Those uncs scary. We openin' up a bowling alley, a family spot.

SHORTY (*LAUGHS*): A bowling alley? You trippin . . . Niggas don't bowl.

QUAN: George Branham III . . . PBA world champion . . . twenty-three perfect games . . . made $747,138 in his professional career . . . an' he started bowling when he was six, jus' like me when Omar started takin' me to Lucky Strikes.

SHORTY: You make money bowlin'?

QUAN: You go professional. You get on the tour. An' you get sponsors. I'm goin' to Lucky Strikes tonight, open 'til 2:00.

SHORTY: I go bowlin' an' I got to rent those smelly, faggy-ass shoes an' my balls rollin' down the gutter.

QUAN pulls a pair of Dexter Brunswick Flyers out of his backpack.

QUAN: Now these is not faggy-ass shoes. They hundred-dollar Brunswick Flyers. The shoes of champions. Bowlin' takes a lot of work bro. It ain't as easy as it looks. You got to get the axis jus' right on your rotation . . . create your own geometrical construction on the platform . . . you got to focus all yer positive energy on the spot you want to hit. It's an art . . .

SHORTY: Ain't no bitch I know wants to go out with a bowler.

QUAN: . . . or a punk neither.

Act II, Scene I
BENEATH THE SYSTEM

---

*Night. Gunshots are heard. The gunshots are followed by
banging sounds, not unlike the shots. Lights up on the cell.
OMAR is asleep on his bunk. A bang on his wall.*

OMAR: What's up?

PRISONER *(FROM THE OTHER SIDE OF THE WALL)*: Send your
line over. I'm gunna send you the newspaper. It got an
article about the hood you need to read.

OMAR: I get it in the morning . . .

PRISONER *(FROM THE OTHER SIDE OF THE WALL)*: You gotta
get it now.

OMAR: A'ight. Give me a minute to put my line together.

*OMAR pulls out a line made of torn sheets. He twirls the
soap in a lasso motion and tosses it into the hall.*

OMAR: You got it?

PRISONER *(FROM THE OTHER SIDE OF THE WALL)*: Yeah. Give
me a minute. Go 'head. Pull it.

*OMAR pulls the line until he retrieves a newspaper tied
to the line. He unties the paper and sits down with it,
just holding it, not reading. He opens the paper and flips
through it. Suddenly stops. He has found the article. QUAN
appears in a tight spot and flatly speaks what OMAR reads.*

QUAN *(ADDRESSING THE AUDIENCE IN A FLAT MONOTONE)*:
The Newark Police Department is investigating a

homicide, the 112th this year, which occurred late Friday night in the parking lot of the Lucky Strikes bowling alley in downtown Newark. Officers responding to reports of a shooting at 2 a.m. found Quan Moore, 22, suffering from a gunshot wound to the stomach. A second shooting victim, Theo "Shorty" Terrell, 24, who was with Moore at the time of the shooting, traveled to University Hospital where he was treated for a minor gunshot wound and released. Moore, who was transported to University Hospital by ambulance, died early Tuesday morning. Anyone with information is asked to call Newark Crime Stoppers at 1-877-NWK-TIPS.

Long beat.

INTERMISSION

Act II, Scene II
FLOATIN'/CHIMENE'S LIGHT DIMS

Projection: ZAIRE at ten.

Morning. A social worker enters the cell.

SOCIAL WORKER: Your request for a funeral visit has been approved. Sign here. This is the $800 charge to your account for the officers' overtime and the vehicle fee.

OMAR signs the form.

SOCIAL WORKER: This is the breakdown of the costs. You leave in ten minutes. Get dressed. Don't make any calls or your trip gets terminated. The administration doesn't want you to go so don't do anything stupid, they'll bring you back, still charge you and toss you in the hole for a week.

OMAR: I know the drill. I jus' want to say goodbye to my brother.

SOCIAL WORKER exits. OMAR hurriedly washes his face and hands in the sink. He puts on his clean khaki clothes, a clean pair of sneakers and brushes his hair. The shift changes. The door locks. OMAR rushes to the gate.

OMAR, SHOUTING: Yo! Bust sixty-three.

The door lock opens. OMAR walks outside.

OJORE: Stay strong, bro.

OMAR approaches a GUARD.

OMAR: Omar Moore, 807209 B.

GUARD: You should have been out before the count.

The following happens during the GUARD's speech. The corrections officer motions for OMAR to strip, but after OMAR pulls off his shirt and is about to remove his pants the corrections officer motions for OMAR to leave them on. The corrections officer does a quick pat-down. OMAR's legs are shackled. He is handcuffed. A chain is put around his waist. The lock for the waist chain is secured in the middle of his back. The officer puts the black box on the cuffs between OMAR's hands to cover the short piece of chain and the key holes. OMAR tries to twist his hands as they are uncomfortable. The GUARD takes his arm and walks him out.

GUARD 1: You get five minutes. No one is allowed in the funeral home while you are there except the funeral director. We see anyone outside we don't like the trip is terminated and you will be brought back. You call out to anyone or motion to anyone on the street and the trip is terminated an' you will be brought back. If your family shows up and tries to see you the trip is terminated and you will be brought back. You tell 'em to stay away?

OMAR: Yes.

The scene shifts. OMAR is facing the audience up stage. The two corrections officers wait in the background. CHIMENE and SHARONDA are in the apartment. They are dressed for the funeral. All are on stage together.

GUARD ONE: Five minutes. We'll be here the whole time.

OMAR, hands and feet shackled, is standing in front of QUAN's open casket. Long silence.

SHARONDA: He should be with Quan now.

CHIMENE: An' we six blocks away. Can't we at least see him come out?

SHARONDA: No, Mommy. He doesn't get to go in if we there.

OMAR (*IN A WHISPER*)**:** Quan . . .

SHARONDA: Quan hated selling the drugs, Mommy . . . scared sick . . . most of it was Shorty . . . he wanted to make sure you had your medicine. He wanted a lawyer for Omar . . . an' we behind on the rent . . . Poor Zaire. First Omar. Now Quan. Zaire hasn't said more than two words since Quan died. All I can do is go up and hold him . . .

OMAR: Little bro . . .

SHARONDA: Denise come by this morning. She brought this.

SHARONDA pulls out a crumpled twenty-dollar bill.

SHARONDA: She say to tell you sorry . . . no mother should have to go what you go through . . . she prayin' for us and Zaire. She said she'd come back when she was more presentable. She loves that boy, mommy. She wears that mother-son ring 'round her neck. It's jus' the drug too strong . . .

CHIMENE says nothing. JIMMY walks into the apartment. He is wearing an oversized suit. He is sober. He walks over and puts his arms around CHIMENE.

OMAR: I should have been there for you. I wasn't there.

JIMMY: I should have been there for that boy. I'm sorry Chimene.

CHIMENE: You here now . . .

JIMMY: I'm his father . . .

OMAR: I'm your big bro . . .

CHIMENE: I'm glad you here, Jimmy. You look nice . . . (*she begins to hum*).

JIMMY: We all go together . . . hold each other up.

OMAR: Forgive me, little bro . . . I'll do better with Zaire.

GUARD (*FROM OUTSIDE THE DOOR*): Two minutes. Say your goodbyes.

OMAR bends over and kisses QUAN.

CHIMENE and JIMMY sing.

CHIMENE AND JIMMY:
> Oh, precious Lord, take my hand
> Lead me on, let me stand I am tired, I am weak, I am
> > worn
> Through the storm, through the night
> Lead me on through the light
> Take my hand, precious Lord
> And lead me home

SHARONDA: The minister be there soon . . . (*hesitantly*) . . . Mommy, are we created to suffer?

CHIMENE (*AFTER A PAUSE*): Is there any love that isn't?

OMAR: I love you, little bro. You was the best of all of us . . . (*Softly*) . . . Bye, Quan.

CHIMENE AND JIMMY, JOINED BY OMAR AND SHAKY BROWN (*SINGING*): Through the storm, through the night / Lead me on through the light / Take my hand, precious Lord / And lead me home

OMAR, JIMMY, and SHARONDA exit, CHIMENE lags behind singing. OMAR stops just before exiting to take one final look at QUAN. He and CHIMENE see each other. Lights down.

Act II, Scene III

DEATH OF CHIMENE

Afternoon. SLASH peeks in OJORE's cell and spots him laying on his bunk.

SLASH (*LOOKING AROUND*): As-Salamu Alaikim.

OJORE: Wa-laykum As-Salam.

SLASH: Where young'en, . . . yard?

OJORE: Naw.

SLASH: I heard the news about his lil' bro . . . this my firs' time getting over here. I wanted to holler at him to see how he was doing. Ojore slowly gets off the bunk and make his way to the door

OJORE (*WHISPERING*): I don't want that nosy nigga in the cell next to me in our conversation . . . Look in there and see what he doin'.

SLASH (*LEANING BACK ON THE GATE TO GET A BETTER LOOK IN THE CELL*): He ain't in there . . . Why . . . What's up?

OJORE (*IN A LOW VOICE*): Yeah, young'en's moms died last Friday.

SLASH: He jus' lost his brother.

OJORE: Yeeeaaah . . . they called him to social services Monday . . . never came back. Second shift told me to pack an overnight bag . . . I ain't heard nothin' since.

SLASH: That's a lot of loss . . . he gonna hold up?

OJORE (*SHAKING HIS HEAD*): Stuff like this break the best of 'em.

SLASH: Word . . . Keep me posted . . . The pig waving me off the tier.

BREAKING THE CODE, OR RADICAL LOVE (RE)EMERGES

Projection: ZAIRE at twelve.

Late afternoon. In the cell. OJORE lays on his bunk reading Martin & Malcom & America *by James Cone. OMAR stares quietly out the small cell window.*

OJORE (*WITHOUT PUTTING THE BOOK DOWN*): How you holdin' up?

OMAR *(IN A FLAT TONE)*: I'm good.

OJORE: You got a letter over there from your sister . . . You gonna write her back?

OMAR: Ummmmhuh.

OJORE: I'm sure she wants to hear from ya.

Pause.

OMAR: I don't have no words . . . no feelings . . .

OJORE hands OMAR SHARONDA's letter.

OJORE: Look son, this is the third letter she wrote you haven't opened, and this one from the county. I think you should try an' look at it. Ain't been easy on her either . . . you got to call your son. It's important.

OMAR: Haven't seen my son in months . . . I got nothing to say . . .

OJORE (*SOFTLY*): That's the cell talkin'. I died in that very same spot over fifteen years ago when the police shot my only son in the back. I had already lost my mama, my pops, even my brothers and sisters stop coming. Five years usually the limit . . . then everyone goes their own way . . . But jus' because yer family doesn't visit doesn't mean they don't love you . . . I ain't gonna lie, when I heard my boy died I wanted to run out of this cell and stab the first pig I saw . . . I laid on that floor for three days . . . All I could do was cry . . . why? . . . why? . . . why? . . . after three days of laying there crying I heard a voice say, "because you can handle it." An' young brother, you can handle it. It ain't gonna be easy . . . but you can get through it . . . you jus' have to find your strength, have to hang onto that love.

OMAR *(NUMB)***:** How I do dat?

OJORE: Be hurt . . . feel . . . then you can heal . . . The soul is like bones, if it ain't set right it won't heal right. Grieve, son . . . grieve, grieve, grieve. The whole point of this system is to make you numb. Once you can't feel, you can't act. You lose your humanity. You become an animal.

Pause.

OJORE: Look, hope's a funny thing. It ain't based on what's real. Us revolutionaries back in the day knew we was doomed. But we couldn't stand by and watch our people get gunned down, the assassination of our leaders. We went underground to fight state-sponsored terrorism, to fight for something beyond ourselves. Most of us were captured . . . a lot of us were killed. An' we still locked up. But the killings by the pigs slowed down. They got scared. It didn't stop . . . but it slowed. We answered aggression with aggression. I ain't sayin' that was right. I'm sayin' they didn't offer us a choice.

OMAR (*FLAT*): Times different now, Ojore.

OJORE: I know that son. Did we fail? Look at me. Two life bids . . . family gone . . . but you know the day I got caught outside that bank . . . began to shoot back . . . watched the pigs run for cover . . . I knew I was the freest Black man in America.

OMAR (*FLAT*): People don't think like that no more.

OJORE: True son, true, but that don't mean I'm wrong. I know this. We born into struggle. It ain't a struggle we can win, but it is one we have to fight, an' to fight it we have to be able to feel what others feel.

OMAR (*FLAT*): I ain't got much left to live for.

OJORE: You got Zaire. You can't save yourself if you stay alone, Omar. You got to connect . . . focus on something bigger than yourself. Alone they'll crush you. An' once you numb, you lost. I ain't gonna let you slip away, son . . . close your eyes, Omar . . . see your mom's face . . . think of your boy . . .

OMAR remains slumped over on his bed. OJORE goes over and lifts him up and holds him by his shoulders. OMAR tries to free himself from OJORE's grasp unsuccessfully.

OJORE: They not goin' turn you into one of their drugged-out zombies, sleep all day and shuffle with the shakes down to the mess hall . . . they ain't winnin' this one. You gonna feel this hurt, boy . . . I know it's hard . . . love's hard . . . yer moms loved you, Omar . . . we got to keep that love.

SHAKY BROWN begins to play.

SHAKY BROWN (*SINGING*): I got a letter this mornin', how do you reckon it read? / It said, "Hurry, hurry, yeah, your love is dead" / I got a letter this mornin', I say how do you reckon it read? / You know, it said, / "Hurry, hurry, how come the gal you love is dead?" / So, I grabbed up my suitcase, and took off down the road/When I got there she was layin' on a coolin' board I grabbed up my suitcase, and I said and I took off down the road I said, but when I got there she was already layin on a coolin' / Well, I walked up right close, looked down in her face / Said, the good ol' gal got to lay here 'til the Judgment Day / I walked up right close, and I said I looked down in her face / I said the good ol' gal, she got to lay here 'til the Judgment Day.

OJORE: He playin' for you, son.

OMAR, still in OJORE's grip, lowers his head. He begins to weep and heave. OJORE continues to hold him by the shoulders.

OJORE: Let it out, son . . . let it out.

OJORE lets go of OMAR and turns to face where the music is coming from.

OJORE: Play, John "Shaky" Brown . . . play . . . keep those slavers away from this boy . . . break these chains . . . turn ol' Satan back to hell.

SHAKY BROWN (*SINGING*): You know, love's a hard ol' fall, make you do things you don't wanna do / Love sometimes leaves you feeling sad and blue / You know, love's a hard ol' fall, make you do things you don't wanna do / Love sometimes make you feel sad and blue . . .

Lights down.

Act II, Scene V
THE SYSTEM STRIKES BACK

Morning. SHARONDA, *in prison khakis, in a spotlight.*

SHARONDA: Dear Omar, I got locked up in the county for forty-four days for the fines on that old DUI. Zaire with Sadiye. I been able to talk to him. That boy don't need this on top of everything else. It's breakin' my heart.

I thought when they pulled me over and told me I had jail time it was a scare tactic. My license had been restored, but it don't make no difference. That shitty public defender told me I had to plead guilty. I'll be out in two weeks. Fuck it.

The guards made me cut my weave so now I wear a headscarf. At least they let me keep my nose ring. Big Bro there's a lot of cryin' in here . . . cryin' for mistakes, cryin' for children mostly. The hardest is listen' to women talk to their kids on the phone. We all feel that shit.

I wish you'd uv warned me about the food. It smells like vomit. I'm trying to get a diet tray. I think they are vegetarian . . . come on blue trays . . . look like clumps of Play-Doh. The meals on the brown trays look like dog food. I collect sugar and juice packets to trade for snacks.

Most of the women in my pod in here for boosting. Or they got high, violated probation, or had a DWI. I don't understand why they can't serve their time under house arrest, especially if they got children.

I had no idea how special it is to have all of your teeth

in jail! Brushing your teeth is showing off!

My bunky is pregnant. When she has to pee she pushes the call button. The pig yells into the speaker, "I will break your fingers if you push that button again." She pees in a milk carton.

My paperwork is messed up. This jail is sayin' I owe $600. A clerical error is keeping me from getting' commissary. My boyfriend is trying to fix it. I feel for those in here who don't have anyone.

The showers here is filled with fruit flies. Swarms of 'em. An' I don't ever want to drop my soap in the showers with the dirt, blood, hair and God only knows what else is in the puddles on the floor. Flip-flops are called suicide shoes. You will slip and damn near kill yourself. Oh, an' don't grab for the shower curtain, it's covered in mold. Speaking of the shower curtain, it's too small. It's a free peep show.

I don't know how you get used to the water comin' out in one-minute spurts and pressin' the button to turn it back on. That takes skills. An' it's lukewarm or cold. What's with the no name brand antibacterial soap? If you ain't light then it makes you ashy.

I stay awake at night. The bunk is too small and hard. I wait 'til I'm exhausted and pass out, which is around three. Count time is at four. Breakfast at six-thirty. I usually get up to pee then, because I know the door will be opened. I go back to sleep until the chatter in the pod becomes unbearable.

I call the plastic box for commissary the treasure chest. Mine is empty. My hair is so fucked up under this scarf. I can't wait to buy shampoo.

Most of the women in here spend time writing judges, pleading with them to keep kids from being adopted. It doesn't seem to do much good. There is a woman in here who watched her man get killed and was locked up the same night. There are women who were told they were being released but still sitting here weeks later. It's sad. I miss Mommy . . . I miss Quan . . . I miss you Omar. I even miss Daddy. I really miss Zaire, I feel like I lost control of him. Now he's takin' it out on the world that took his daddy away . . .

Medical is fucked up. They won't give a woman in here naproxen for her endometriosis . . . naproxen cost money and the medical company in here to make money not spend it . . . her sheets soaked with blood . . . she's in a lot of pain. Medical gave her Motrin and charged her account. She's too weak and dizzy to walk.

Bitches do strange things for change. Feel me? Monsters walk the halls at night, stand outside a cell and start yellin', sayin' the woman inside smokin' just so they can enter the cells. The jailhouse relationships intense! Girls on girls. They be drainin' the toilet pipes to talk all night to their man downstairs. You should hear that chatter. The freaks really come out in the dark. This one girl so loud an' she never stops talkin' . . . day and night. She be, 'Hey, blah blah blah.' She talkin' to different men, which you definitely don't do. She a ho, on the bowl. Bowl phone love. Crazy.

A girl named Krystina lost her son today. She been cryin' all day on her bunk. He was adopted by a rich white woman who can't have children . . . it's a cold world. The men go to prison an' their mothers, sisters, wives an' girlfriends take care of them. Send them money for commissary . . . visit. But women in prison on their own. They lose everyone, even their kids.

Write Zaire, Omar. An' write me. I know you got stamps. Love you, big bro, Sharonda.

Act II, Scene VI

SHAKY GROUND

Morning.

OJORE: Peace, brother. You a'ight?

OMAR: It come up.

OJORE: How you know?

OMAR: The transfer log . . . name on the list . . . on his way. Push be in this prison soon . . . an' he got my brother's blood on his hands.

OJORE: Ya mind made up?

OMAR: I got my shank. An' I know who it's for . . .

OJORE nods gravely.

OJORE: Shankin' Push ain't bringin' back Quan. I wish you'd bury that shank and keep your eyes on gettin' out . . . Besides, most of that prison code a fiction. Lot of guys in here look the other way.

OMAR: I decided this a long time ago, Ojore.

OJORE: Well son, I'll tell you what to prepare for. When they come and get you, 'cause they are gonna get you, have your hands out in front of you with your palms showing. You want them to see you have no weapons. Don't make no sudden moves. Put your hands behind your head. Drop to your knees as soon as they begin barking out commands.

OMAR: My knees?

OJORE: This ain't a debate. I'm telling you how to survive.

When you get to the hole you ain't gonna be allowed to see nobody or have nothing.

OMAR: Why?

OJORE: 'Cause they don't want you sendin' messages to nobody before dey question da brothers on the wing. IA gonna come and see you . . . gonna want a statement. The pigs gonna let the cold in . . . gonna mess with ya food . . . gonna wake you up every hour so you can't sleep . . . gonna use the dogs . . . gonna put a spotlight in front of ya cell . . . gonna harass you wit' all kinds of threats . . . gonna send in the turtles . . . give you beatdowns . . . maybe a dry cell . . . no water unless they feel like turnin' it on.

OMAR: How long?

OJORE: Til they break you . . . 'til they don't . . . three days . . . three weeks . . . if you don't think you can take it, then don't start puttin' yerself through this hell . . . tell 'em what they wanna know from the door. You gonna be in MCU for the next two or three years. You lookin' at a life bid. They wait for you to self-destruct . . . self-mutilate . . . paranoia . . . panic attacks . . . hearing voices . . . hallucinations. I seen one man swallow a pack of AA batteries. Then you get restraint hoods, restraint belts, restraint beds, waist and leg chains. I seen a lot of men break.

Pause.

OJORE: You ready? You sure this is what you want?

OMAR: I ain't livin' in this prison with Push.

OJORE: I feel you, son. I feel you. But if you think you gonna regret it, don't do it.

OMAR: I may not see you for a while, Ojore.

OJORE: Yeah, quite a while you do this.

OMAR: Malcolm, George Jackson, they comin' with me.

OJORE: I had long talks with Brother Jackson. Could almost see him sittin' in the cell. Stay strong, Omar.

They shake hands.

Lights dim.

Act II, Scene VII

HUMANITY TRIUMPHS

Projection: Zaire at fourteen.

Late afternoon. Omar is standing outside the mess hall.

Noise of men, dishes, chairs. Slash enters.

Slash: What's up, young'en.

Omar: What's up.

Slash: Let me holla at you for a minute.

Omar walks over to Slash.

Omar: What's happening?

Slash (*whispering*): I know you going in there to stab that boy they say killed ya brother . . .

Omar: Yeah.

Slash: Yeah, the whole prison know it.

Omar: Word?

Slash: You don't think he know what's up?

Omar: I don't give a fuck what he know!

Slash: Well I give a fuck what he know cuz dem niggas he eating with . . .

Pause.

Slash: Ain't sitting with him for nothin' . . . They with him 'cause they watching his back. I watched him put his team together the moment he walked in here . . . cuz in his mind, he got to kill you 'fore you kill him.

OMAR: He fuckin' right he gotta kill me! That nigga killed my brother. And I don't give a fuck who wit' him! They can get it too!

The two stare at each other intently.

SLASH: Yeah, I can dig it . . . I know you wanna kill that nigga and that feeling ain't promise to ever go away.

Pause.

SLASH: But I know one thing . . . you gonna wanna get out of here one day . . . an' if you kill that nigga you ain't never leavin' this prison.

OMAR: I don't give a fuck.

SLASH: You don't give a fuck now . . .

OMAR: That's right! How you know I got a shank? Ojore?

SLASH: I'm doin' this fer yer pops, who isn't here to do it himself. He done lost one son. That's enough. Slip me the shank. Any shankin' to be done be done by me. I'm gonna die in here one way or another. But 'neither of us shankin' that boy. 'Nough blood and hate as it is. I ain't sayin' you got to forgive 'em, but ya got to let him live. He be dyin' in here wit me. An' it's Uncle Bip's job to see you get out. One of us gonna have a life.

Pause.

OMAR: Quan wasn't cuttin' into his game . . . he could barely sell anything once I got locked up. Push took Quan out 'cause of me. Quan's death my fault. This the least I can do . . . I don't matter no more.

SLASH: You got yer son. You got yer sister . . .

OMAR: They don't hardly come and when they do my boy sit and sulk. He tired of me preachin' to him from behind a plexiglas wall or on the phone. I wasn't able to be a father to him . . . I tried . . . but he sees I'm powerless. He do what he want. He angry . . . an' he got every right to be angry.

SLASH: You do this you'll never get out, . . . you'll never be a father.

OMAR: Zaire be a man when I get out.

SLASH: That don't mean he don't need you, Omar. I know the code says you got to shank him. But that's the public code. There's another code. It says he stay away from you an' you stay away from him . . . he a phantom . . . you a phantom . . . and there's more people than you think playin' by this code . . .

OMAR: I can't be livin' in here with Push.

SLASH: You know how I got my life sentence?

OMAR (*COLDLY*): Naw.

OMAR starts to walk away. SLASH blocks him and grabs his shoulder. It is clear SLASH will, if he has to, use force to stop OMAR from going into the mess hall.

SLASH: You think I came to jail with a life sentence? Fuck no! I came in here like you . . . doing about a dime and I run into a nigga did something to my family. Yeah, an' I thought I had to do something to that nigga to make a statement . . . prove I wasn't a weak motherfucker . . . huh so I could live freely in a goddamn prison.

OMAR: That ain't why I'm doing it. I don't give a fuck what these niggas think.

SLASH: It don't matter why you doin' it, the fact is you gonna do it . . . jus' like I did it . . . Yeah, I stabbed a nigga in that mess hall twenty years ago an' he died. I remember standing there . . . watching him bleed to death. The shit didn't even feel real . . . like a dream. All the sound sucked out of the world . . . silence . . . all I could do was close my eyes and cry . . . Then I heard this voice screaming "WHAT THE FUCK DID YOU DO? WHAT THE FUCK DID YOU DO?" . . . spent over a year in the ad. seg. 'fore I realized that voice was mine. When I killed that nigga, it drove me crazy! Now I'm doing life in this shit hole! I watched a lot of dumb niggas come and go, but I've been here ever since . . . listening to the same sounds, wearing the same clothes, looking at these same walls, eatin' the same shit in that same mess hall where I lost my god damn mind . . . I'm trapped in time . . . For what? Killing a nigga that was already dead . . . Push got life! I know what that's like . . . Give me that shank young'en . . . Ya brother dead and that nigga dead! Case closed, all I can do now is try to save yo' life. Give me the shank . . . Don't go in that mess hall. I'll send some food over to ya wing and we'll figure this shit out tomorrow but right now I need you to hand me that shank.

OMAR: Slash, you know I can't walk away from this . . .

SLASH: Yeah you can . . . Come to Jum'ah with me Friday . . . don't matter what you believe in . . . when you line up in a row with the other brothers your gonna get their strength . . . feel their spirit! An' you gone need it! You gonna need a lot of it, 'cause you still got a while 'fore you get outta here. An' I'm gone make sure you get outta here . . . hear me? Give me the shank, Omar.

OMAR stares at SLASH. He slowly reaches up his sleeve and passes the shank to SLASH in what looks like a hand shake and embrace. Lights down.

MAKING PEACE/TAKING LOSSES

Projection: ZAIRE at nineteen.

Afternoon. Downtown Newark. OMAR is wearing a baggy white T-shirt, gray sweatpants, and white Reebok sneakers. He is carrying a white net laundry bag over his shoulder with papers and pictures. He sees his father in soiled clothes slumped against a wall.

OMAR: Pop . . . Pop (shaking him) . . . Pop?

JIMMY (*COMING OUT OF HIS NOD*): Heeeey huh, Omar?

OMAR: Yeah, it's me, Pop.

JIMMY: Damn, so they finally let you out . . . Man, I ain't think I was gone ever see you again. I couldn't believe they got you . . . Ya Momma cried for weeks after Quan got killed. I guess she couldn't take it, ' specially after the eviction . . .

OMAR (*GENTLY*): How you holding up?

JIMMY: I guess I'm pretty fair. I'm pretty fair.

OMAR: Yeah . . . You know I thought about you a lot while I was gone. Whenever somebody from the hood came through I'd ask about you . . . I missed you, Pop.

JIMMY: Yeah, it's been kinda rough out here after yer momma died.

OMAR: I know. But . . . we can get through this together . . .

JIMMY: Yeah, man, but uuh you look like you doing ok.

OMAR: Just glad to be home.

JIMMY: Uuuummhuh. I know you got a couple dollars you could let me have.

OMAR takes a long look at his father.

OMAR: Naw, I ain't got no money. I'm jus' trying to figure out how I'm gonna make it . . . need to find my boy . . .

JIMMY: I know you gonna come up with something!

OMAR: I don't have no choice.

JIMMY: Yeah, yeah, you right about that . . . you sure you ain't got a couple dollars?

OMAR: Naw, man but it's good to see you. (*OMAR gives his father an awkward hug.*) I'm gonna take off.

JIMMY: Oh ok . . . you know me . . . I'll stand the test of time . . . I'll be a'ight.

OMAR: Stay up, Pop.

JIMMY, looking up with difficulty, drifts in and out.

Coda

ECHO

———

This is a reprise of Act I, Scene II. The light should be different. Lights dim.

CHIMENE is in a rocker, singing to a toddler in his bed.

CHIMENE (*SINGING*):

> Go down, Moses
> Way down in Egypt land
> Tell all pharaohs to
> Let my people go!
> When Israel was in Egypt land
> Let my people go!
> Oppressed so hard they could not stand
> Let my people go!

SHARONDA walks into the room quietly.

CHIMENE:

> So the God said: Go down, Moses
> Way down in Egypt land
> Tell all pharaohs to
> Let my people go!
> So Moses went to Egypt land
> Let my people go!
> He made all pharaohs understand
> Let my people go!

SHARONDA and CHIMENE speaking quietly.

SHARONDA: Zaire asleep?

CHIMENE: I think so.

SHARONDA: I love hearin' you sing, Mama.

CHIMENE: My grandma sang this to me. An' her grandma sang it to her. An' before that a mama, blood of my blood, sang it to her little girl or boy growin' up in slavery . . . an' all these mamas had to fight the evil in the world was love . . . an' song . . .

A police siren is heard outside. CHIMENE walks to the window and looks outside.

CHIMENE: Omar home?

SHARONDA: Not yet. We got to wait? I'm gettin' hungry. You never know when he get here.

CHIMENE: He be here soon.

The light rises faintly on SHAKY BROWN's cell and he joins CHIMENE in the song.

> Yes, the Lord said: Go down, Moses
> Way down in Egypt land
> Tell all pharaohs to
> Let my people go!

The light in SHAKY BROWN's cell dims to darkness.

Sound of a door opening downstairs. SHARONDA leaves.

OMAR (OS): Ma?

Lights out.

END OF PLAY

GLOSSARY

AD. SEG.—Administrative segregation where a prisoner is held for lengthy periods of isolation for institutional infractions.

A BUNDLE—Ten bags of heroin.

BUCK FIFTY—A knife cut running from the ear to the lips. It is inflicted on prisoners that use the phone without the permission of the gang member that controls the phone. Buck fifty refers to the number of stitches.

CRAF—Central Reception Assignment Facility. Where prisoners are first processed and held before being assigned a permanent cell.

CASED UP—Charged by the police.

CO—Correction Officer.

CODE SIXTY-SIX—A medical emergency.

CUSTY—Slang for customers.

G PACK—$1,000 worth of drugs.

THE HOLE—Where prisoners are first sent for pre-hearing detention for committing infractions in prison. Prisoners in the hole are not permitted to have any personal property or phone privileges. They are held in the hole for between five and thirty days before being returned to the general population or transferred to administrative segregation.

IRON PILE—Weightlifting equipment.

IA—Internal Affairs is made up of Department of Corrections staff that investigate correctional officers for infractions.

JACK MACK—Pouched mackerel available from the prison commissary.

JUM'AH—The Muslim prayer on Friday.

LOCKDOWN—When there is no movement permitted to the prisoners within the prison because of an emergency or incident.

MCU—Management Control Unit. It was created in Scarborough State Prison in 1975 for prisoners who had not broken prison rules, but who were, because of their political beliefs, deemed to be a threat by prison administrators. It was first used to quarantine members of the Black Panthers and the Black Liberation Army. Prisoners in the MCU spend up to twenty-three hours a day in their cells, are isolated, under constant surveillance, and have their correspondence and reading material heavily censored. It is, in essence, a prison within the prison.

OLD HEAD—Older prisoners who come out of an older prison culture where there is more respect given to fellow prisoners and a stronger sense of loyalty.

ROCK—The cooked up, hard form of cocaine.

RUNNER—A prisoner allowed to carry out duties such as cleaning the tiers, passing out cleaning supplies, and handing out juice or trays.

SHANK—An improvised knife made out of metal, plastic, or other material.

SNITCH—Informant.

STASH—Where drugs or a body is hidden.

TIER—The row of cells on a block that can be four stories, or tiers, high.

TURTLES, ALSO KNOWN AS NINJAS—Members of the Prison SOG (Special Operations Group), the prison's version of a SWAT team. The SOG teams, which handle disturbances in the prison, wear black uniforms, body armor, helmets with visors, shin guards, forearms pads, and are equipped with gas masks. They carry batons, shields, and pepper spray.

UNCS—Older male junkies. Older female junkies are called aunties.

In New Jersey, a life sentence is natural life. It does not include a set number of years. When a prisoner is eligible for parole it means he or she has completed a mandatory minimum sentence or required time served. The prisoner is then at the mercy of a parole board that can grant parole or deny it. Going before a parole board does not mean one will be freed. Very few prisoners are paroled when they first become eligible.

ABOUT THE AUTHORS

THE NEW JERSEY PRISON THEATER COOPERATIVE is a committee that includes not only the twenty-eight formerly incarcerated participants but also six theater professionals, who worked on the script's development.

CHRIS HEDGES is a Pulitzer Prize–winning journalist. He is the author of the bestsellers *American Fascists* and *Days of Destruction, Days of Revolt,* and was a National Book Critics Circle finalist for *War Is a Force That Gives Us Meaning.* He teaches in college credit courses in prisons in New Jersey. His most recent book, *Our Class: Trauma and Transformation in an American Prison* tells the story behind the writing of *Caged.*

BORIS FRANKLIN, the author of *The Poetic Side of a Man's Mind,* served eleven years in prison from 2004 to 2015. He sits on the board of the New Jersey Prison Reentry Program as well as the Mountain View Community Student Advisory Board. He is a visiting fellow at the Global Center for Advance Studies.

ABOUT HAYMARKET BOOKS

Haymarket Books is a radical, independent, nonprofit book publisher based in Chicago.

Our mission is to publish books that contribute to struggles for social and economic justice. We strive to make our books a vibrant and organic part of social movements and the education and development of a critical, engaged, international left.

We take inspiration and courage from our namesakes, the Haymarket martyrs, who gave their lives fighting for a better world. Their 1886 struggle for the eight-hour day—which gave us May Day, the international workers' holiday—reminds workers around the world that ordinary people can organize and struggle for their own liberation. These struggles continue today across the globe—struggles against oppression, exploitation, poverty, and war.

Since our founding in 2001, Haymarket Books has published more than five hundred titles. Radically independent, we seek to drive a wedge into the risk-averse world of corporate book publishing. Our authors include Noam Chomsky, Arundhati Roy, Rebecca Solnit, Angela Y. Davis, Howard Zinn, Amy Goodman, Wallace Shawn, Mike Davis, Winona LaDuke, Ilan Pappé, Richard Wolff, Dave Zirin, Keeanga-Yamahtta Taylor, Nick Turse, Dahr Jamail, David Barsamian, Elizabeth Laird, Amira Hass, Mark Steel, Avi Lewis, Naomi Klein, and Neil Davidson. We are also the trade publishers of the acclaimed Historical Materialism Book Series and of Dispatch Books.

ALSO AVAILABLE FROM HAYMARKET BOOKS

Freedom Is a Constant Struggle
Ferguson, Palestine, and the Foundations of a Movement
Angela Y. Davis, edited by Frank Barat, preface by Cornel West

The Brother You Choose: Panthers, Politics, and Revoltuion
Paul Coates and Eddie Conway, edited by Susie Day, introduction by
Ta-Nehisi Coates

The Long Term: Resisting Life Sentences Working Toward Freedom
Edited by Alice Kim, Erica Meiners, Jill Petty, Audrey Petty,
Beth E. Richie, and Sarah Ross

Reading Revolution: Shakespeare on Robben Island
Ashwin Desai

Six by Ten: Stories from Solitary
Edited by Mateo Hoke and Taylor Pendergrass

This Is Modern Art: A Play
Kevin Coval and Idris Goodwin

A Time to Die: The Attica Prison Revolt
Tom Wicker